Philosophy for Children

Thinking about thinking in the early years.

By

Marilyn Bowles

'Thinking skills enable children and young people to reason, question, predict, think independently and develop their capacity for reflection and judgement. Creative thinking skills can help children and young people understand their own capabilities and qualities as an active learner. This creative approach contributes to the emotional and social development and well-being of all young people, including those with disabilities. Philosophy for Children is an approach which advocates setting up a community of enquiry as an interactive method of discussion.'

National Children's Bureau

Published 2008 by A & C Black Publishers Limited
38 Soho Square, London W1D 3HB
www.acblack.com

First published 2008 by Featherstone Education Limited

ISBN 978-1-906029-21-0

Text © Marilyn Bowles 2008
Photographs © Kerry Ingham 2008

A CIP record for this publication is available from the British Library.

Printed in Malta by Gutenberg Press Limited

This book is produced using paper that is made from wood grown in
managed, sustainable forests. It is natural, renewable and recyclable.
The logging and manufacturing processes conform to the environmental
regulations of the country of origin.

To see our full range of titles
visit **www.acblack.com**

Contents

Who is this book for?

This book is for all practitioners working with young children, their managers and advisers, who are all aware of the importance of good speaking, listening and responding skills as a basis for the vital skills of reading and writing. The description 'practitioner' in this book refers to teachers, teaching assistants, nursery nurses and other nursery workers, students and parent helpers willing to get involved in this exciting work. There are many activities which promote communication skills but the 'Community of Enquiry' approach, which is created when philosophical issues are debated by a group of young children, enables them to become deeper thinkers and to extend these creative and critical skills to all areas of their learning, as well as helping them to become better communicators.

The Early Years Foundation Stage Guidance (2008) and the Early Years Profile (2007) identify these skills as essential for lifelong learning.

In Key Stage 1 these developing skills should be supported and extended, growing as children become even more independent and encouraged to collaborate in their learning, particularly when building their skills of speaking and listening.

P4C is a useful strategy for quiet, withdrawn children, who often get left behind in the rapid pace of modern education, where the pace is rapid and the topic may not meet their needs, stage of development or interest. Children who are not encouraged to think 'outside the box' in an imaginative way, high-fliers desperate to try out theories which excite them will also find P4C gives them opportunities to contribute and to expand their thinking.

This book aims to help you to broaden the curriculum, to encourage staff, managers, governors and local authority advisers to look more widely and creatively at their approach to children's learning and to give all concerned the confidence to experiment with language for communication <u>and</u> for thinking.

Introduction

Why philosophy? - the pressures of modern childhood

The current environment

Sue Palmer is a well known writer on the effects of 21st Century life on children's emotional development, and she was part of the group that devised the Primary Literacy Strategy. As she met children and their teachers she discovered that adult assumptions about children's language and literacy skills on entry into school might be inaccurate. She came to the conclusion that many children's communication levels may well be below those of previous generations. She began to investigate why this might have happened, and her research led her to some startling conclusions, which were published in **Toxic Childhood** (2006) and **Detoxing Childhood** (2007).

She suggests that there are at least ten reasons for this worrying reduction in children's speaking, listening and responding skills, which if left unresolved would have a massive impact on reading and writing skills, and inevitably result in a decline in the nation's literacy talent. Her observations led to her to suggest some ways in which this decline could be halted. Of course any intervention should be supported at home and in school - recognising that communication between people is an essential forerunner to acquiring other literacy skills, and that philosophical enquiry could be a key activity in halting linguistic decline.

Diet, additives and supplements

In Jamie Oliver's programmes the majority of parents noticed a huge and positive effect on behaviour when their children ate a diet of healthy food. The improvement disappeared when children reverted to eating junk food and drinking soft drinks full of additives. In separate research children taking regular doses of Omega 3 and Omega 6 fish oil supplements made stunning gains in reading and spelling.

Play

Research discussed in such books as 'Last Child in the Woods' shows that time spent playing in natural environments, such as playing outside in a green space, fostered more creative play, required greater interaction between children and ultimately boosted their communication and thinking skills.

Sleep

Most children are not getting enough sleep. The recommended sleeping time for those aged 4 - 6 years is 10 hours. And a bedtime story, no TV in the room, and regular bedtimes can also help to establish helpful routines which benefit everyone.

Communication

Lack of communication with their parents could be harming children's long term development. All children need conversations, with direct eye contact, with interested people, preferably their parents, so they can learn the importance of talk for understanding, thinking, communicating and learning.

Child care

Pressures on parents, and the need for parents to work, can result in children being left to their own devices, often relying on televisions and computers as companions and babysitters. Out of home child care needs to nurture children's development as much as their mothers and fathers could, so we need the best possible quality of child care.

Education

Pressure on schools for test results and targeting in English and Maths, has resulted in less time for developing other vital life skills for learning, including social, emotional and behavioural skills.

The consumer culture

The use of 'pester power' encouraged by advertising and peer pressure mean that parents can feel blackmailed into buying their children the next 'cool' toy or clothing. A rising incidence of mental illness and depression among the young, has been linked to the pressure to possess.

Technology

Access to computers, e-mail, the internet, 24-hour satellite channels, DVD, mobile phones and computer games is breaking down the close relationships between some parents and their children. Firstly, there's less time spent outdoors, and secondly there's more exposure to potentially damaging influences. We need to move electronic equipment, (such as TV, the Internet and video games) out of children's bedrooms and into family spaces, so parents can safeguard their children and really get to know them.

Politeness and care for others' feelings

'Modern life has eroded good manners. This is a by-product of the increased pace of life, breakdown of the family and the influence of modern technology. Handed-down 'wisdom' of carers, and social support amongst groups of adults is no longer there.'

'All children - even very young ones - can focus for long periods on self-chosen activities (as parents forced to play endless games of peek-a-boo or 'pick up the rattle' know only too well.) However, once children begin to socialise with others, they must learn sometimes to focus on other people's choices; and by six or seven, they're expected to focus on what the teacher is teaching them. If you can't attend - or if you're only prepared to attend to the things that interest you - you're going to have trouble at school.'

'Increasingly, children in general have problems focusing their attention, exercising self-restraint and taking account of other people's needs and interest.'

'But children are not fully developed adults - they still have to move along that developmental continuum, acquiring the habits of civilised behaviour. Focused attention, deferred gratification, self-control, empathy and other important lessons can't be learned at electric speed. Human development happens in 'slow time, and contemporary children need the same time-consuming, old-fashioned nurturing that small, highly intelligent primates have needed through the ages.'

Sue Palmer in 'Toxic Childhood' 2006

Why philosophy? - It's all about thinking

Thinking philosophically helps children to consider questions that include the words what? where? why? how? The Philosophy with Children strategy (P4C) is now practised in more than 30 countries worldwide, and is one of the key ways to develop effective thinking with young children. In philosophy sessions children are encouraged to reason, explain their thinking, listen and build on the ideas of others. This happens within a 'Community of Enquiry' in the setting or classroom, where children sit in a circle with a facilitator (the practitioner). The smaller the group, the more opportunity there will be for everyone to hear and have a chance to speak, so as many adults as possible should work with groups, so the numbers are kept as low as possible.

These supportive and well managed discussions will involve children and adults in thinking of their own ideas and feelings, and grappling with ideas which others suggest.

During P4C discussions, sensitive and complex concepts can arise, and these may include:

- love
- hate
- revenge
- justice
- power
- egality
- freedom
- belief
- friendship
- death
- honesty
- fairness
- loyalty
- courage
- generosity

Philosophical questions are those which have many answers and no 'right' answer. These questions involve possibilities, opinions, variations, and even a change of views.

> Working with a group of children who were debating which of three objects (a carved wooden bowl, a patterned silk scarf, a pear) was the 'odd-one-out' led to a lengthy sharing of wide-ranging views and observations. From the obvious 'You can eat the pear, but you can't eat the bowl or the scarf' to 'The patterns on the scarf and bowl are made by artists, the pattern on the pear is natural'.

> After lots of 'I agree with.............because' and 'I disagree with...........because', we drew the session to a close by asking whether anyone had any questions about the session. This allowed one child to ask 'But which one IS the odd-one-out?'

Philosophy for children is a not an academic field of study only found in books that record centuries of philosophical debate, it lives in everyday, informal philosophy - speaking and listening to each other here and now, thinking and reflecting on ideas - and adults do not need an academic background to try philosophy with children.

Where did the idea come from?

Philosophy for Children was first developed by Professor Matthew Lipman and his associates at the Institute for the Advancement of Philosophy for Children in New Jersey, USA, during the 1960's and 70's as a method of encouraging children to be more reasonable - able to reason and be reasoned with.

P4C work in Great Britain has been supported by the education charity SAPERE which provides training and resources to support anyone working in this field. SAPERE training also promotes the use of art, posters, music and objects or newspapers, in fact anything which can be looked at with fresh eyes in discussion with others.

Initially Lipman used specially constructed stories which he wrote to prompt debate of a variety of dilemmas, and in this country Robert Fisher, Professor at Brunel University has developed the idea of using poetry as well as his own stories to promote discussion. Karin Murris has used a wide range of good picture books very effectively with other carefully selected resources to expand the enquiry approach.

The development of a 'Community of Enquiry' where ideas can be explored through 'Socratic' dialogue, ideas are shared, opinions made and changed and values explored.

Section One - P4C and Current Initiatives
P4C and Every Child Matters (ECM)

Every Child Matters aims to improve the life chances of all children, reducing inequalities and helping them achieve what they want and need out of life. The five outcomes of Every Child Matters are:

1. Be healthy: enjoying good physical and mental health and living a healthy lifestyle.
2. Stay safe: being protected from harm and abuse.
3. Enjoy and achieve: getting the most out of life and developing skills for adulthood.
4. Make a positive contribution: being involved with the community and society and not engaging in anti-social or offending behaviour.
5. Achieve economic well-being: achieving their full potential in life, and not being prevented by economic disadvantage from doing so.

These five outcomes form the basis of the *Every Child Matters* initiative, which leads schools and settings across the whole curriculum. P4C admirably develops outcomes 1, 3 and 4, and in doing so, will also support outcomes 2 and 5.

Social and Emotional Aspects of Learning (SEAL)

A closer look at the SEAL programme shows the importance of philosophical enquiry as a tool. You can find out more about the SEAL programme at the DCSF Standards Site: Social and Emotional Aspects of Learning:

> www.dfes.gov.uk/primary/publications/banda/seal

The social and emotional aspects of learning, are described as - 'The underpinning qualities and skills that help us manage life and learning effectively.'

Self-awareness

- I know when and how I learn most effectively and can recognise when I find something hard to achieve;
- I know that feelings, thoughts and behaviour are linked.

Managing feelings

- I can stop and think before acting;
- I have a range of strategies for managing my worries, other uncomfortable feelings and my anger.

Empathy

- I know that all people have feelings but understand that they might experience and show their feelings in different ways in different circumstances;
- I value and respect the thoughts, feelings, beliefs and values of other people and know that my actions affect other people and can make them feel better of worse.

Motivation

- I can break a long term plan into smaller achievable steps, plan to overcome obstacles, set success criteria and celebrate when I achieve them;
- I can choose when and where to direct my attention, concentrate and resist distractions for increasing periods of time, and how to evaluate my learning and use this to improve future performance.

Social skills

- I can work well in a group, cooperating with others to achieve a joint outcome and I can tell you what helps a group to work well together;
- I can make a wise choice with work or behaviour.

Another essential support appears to be the promotion and provision of 'sustained shared thinking', and what better opportunity for this than in quality time set aside for thinking and discussion.

A community of enquiry needs to be nourished - it cannot spring up overnight. The classroom ethos needs to be appropriate, and adults must build an atmosphere of trust where children can share their thoughts and feelings. The role of the facilitator is to reveal the philosophical issues for discussion, using a variety of stimuli. The children then lead the dialogue, steering it in the direction they choose, with the adult asking questions which help the children to think more deeply and challenge their own and others' assumptions.

'The positive impact of Philosophy for Children at Gallions Primary School in the London Borough of Newham, was highlighted by OFSTED inspectors after a visit in 2006.

> 'The (P4C) lessons reflect the commitment of the staff to producing challenging work for the pupils, but work that enables thinking skills to be used in a variety of circumstances. The P4C lessons throughout the school are skilfully handled with an emphasis on reflection and deeper thought. Such lessons give pupils very good opportunities to express their views on subjects such as their faith, culture and life choices.'
>
> **Ofsted**

Exploring the Intelligences through P4C

What's special about dialogue? Dialogue requires us as adults to shift from being dispensers of information or knowledge to facilitators of learning, and this is easier in the more flexible organisation of the early years. Dialogue is much more than mere conversation, it is the exploring of a theme using resources such as stories, poetry, Artefact, art, film or music while addressing questions such as:

- Can you say more about that?
- How does that make you feel?
- Do you have evidence for that view?
- What makes you say or think that?
- Does anyone else agree with you?

Dialogue between children and their teachers, which stimulates a deeper engagement with an experience or an object, can take the learning to a deeper level of understanding. Dialogue stimulates everyone to pose questions and pursue different perceptions of the truth. Through dialogue we can help children to resolve differences, tolerate diversity and support each other in learning, stimulating higher levels of thinking and creativity. This supports the improvement of specific parts of thinking, and particularly:

Emotional intelligence - self-awareness, self-regulation, motivation, empathy and social skills - all vital to the rounded development of our minds. Young children need to develop these skills alongside all the other areas of their learning.

Spiritual intelligence - includes the widening of vision and confirming of values, seeing connections in life, being able to work against convention and be spontaneously adaptive, becoming richer 'without' and 'within'. Children who take part in these sessions are able to develop listening skills and empathy with others in the group, learn how to be reasonable when sharing ideas, and begin to ask questions of their own to help their learning.

In order to develop dialogue we need to use a range of techniques, setting the scene for dialogue to proceed by:

- asking open questions;
- giving some thinking time;
- listening;
- withholding judgement;
- focusing attention on the speaker;
- not 'putting down' others;
- respecting the views of others;
- being truthful;
- keeping an open mind.

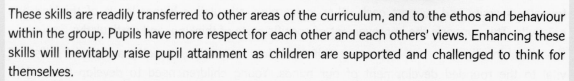

Using these strategies in philosophical enquiry helps children to understand more about how they learn, becoming independent learners and thinkers, using knowledge of themselves to make opinions, evaluate their own behaviour, and as a result, raising their self-esteem and confidence.

These skills are readily transferred to other areas of the curriculum, and to the ethos and behaviour within the group. Pupils have more respect for each other and each others' views. Enhancing these skills will inevitably raise pupil attainment as children are supported and challenged to think for themselves.

The Early Years Foundation Stage Curriculum (2008) highlights the importance attached to sustained shared thinking, transforming understanding, considering challenges and dilemmas, all of which can be supported through P4C.

The Primary National Strategy (2006) also places a strong emphasis on speaking, listening and responding, group discussion and interaction. A fundamental feature of P4C is that everyone has their own story/philosophy and that each person is an expert on their own life.

The Early Years Foundation Stage and KS1
- How does Philosophy for Children relate to the Curriculum?

(The relevant parts of the Foundation Stage Curriculum and the KS1 Core Learning in Literacy are appended in the final section)

The stimulus for philosophical thought in young people should capture their imaginations through poems, stories, interesting objects, music and art, walks of awareness, social dilemmas and current issues, games, dialogues and pictures. Philosophy is a creative exercise, expanding the imagination, self-expression and self-esteem. It helps to develop manners and group empathy in young people as they explore the whole curriculum together. It ensures continuity in the progression of speaking, listening and responding skills.

But thinking philosophically can be scary! It is thinking without a safety net. Some people find this frightening and they like to stay where they feel safe. Others find these big questions hugely exciting. They try, coolly and calmly, to figure out as best they can what's most likely to be true.

Even those things we normally take for granted, such as:

WHY do we have to go to school?

can be open to question and discussion.

Thinking like a detective, sifting the evidence, weighing up arguments, wondering, are all tasks which young minds can enjoy and benefit from.

Matthew Lipman, the founder of philosophy for children, argues that a 'Community of enquiry' should be developed in a particular way. He suggests that pupils should sit in a circle so they can be seen and heard equally. After the initial stimulus; story, object, sounds, whatever it may be the teacher asks 'What interests you about this?' or 'What puzzles you?' or 'What did you like?'

As pupils become more confident with this routine they can decide which question <u>they</u> would like to discuss. Encouraging this ability to make choices and agree priorities takes time, commitment and planning for regular sessions which build on and support other circle time activities.

Philosophy for children follows the ideas of Lev Vygotsky that

'learning to think between people (dialogue) led to the ability to think alone (in the mind).'

1978 'The Mind in Society'

Some basic principles are common to all circle or sharing times are:

- Each person is respected;
- We listen carefully to each other;
- We sometimes help other people to express them selves;
- Each person's views are taken seriously;
- We challenge other people's views respectfully;
- We make sure everyone can contribute.

Refined for younger children these can be:

- One person speaks at a time;
- We look at the person who is speaking;
- We have a reason for what we say.

Following these principles can help children to grow in confidence, and adults to improve their open-ended questioning skills. The principles also allow young people more opportunities to talk, improving speaking, listening and reasoning skills.

Eventually young people can pose their own questions for discussion as well as those that are planned or suggested by adults.

Other possibilities are the idea of being able to change your mind, through thought, discussion, reflection or persuasion by someone else. The idea of persuading others to agree with you through discussion and debate may be new to many children, and should be given plenty of time.

Adult prompts for these sessions could include:

- What reason do you have for saying that?
- Can you explain what you mean?
- Can you give an example?

The adults' role should be that of co-enquirer, never providing answers, just alternative views.

Making a difference.
You may be saying 'But does it really make a difference?'

What the experts say:

'Encouraging young people to think critically about morals and religious questions does not lead to the collapse of moral values.'

Stephen Law, Philosopher; University of London

A recent study in Northumberland showed that young school children can gain greatly from even a small experience of philosophy.

'This doesn't just bring a measurable increase in IQ, it also boosts social skills, because they learn about turn-taking, listening to others carefully and tolerantly. Young people need active learning with hands-on experiences but a quiet, reflective mind is also worthy of development.'

National Teacher Research Conference 2004

A primary school child quoted in the **SAPERE** newsletter Feb. 2006:

'Well, outside of school I feel real. Inside school I don't feel real. Philosophy makes me feel half-real.'

Definitions of Philosophy by Year 6 pupils, in the **SAPERE** newsletter Feb. 2006:

- Saying things that mean something in real life;
- Thinking about things you've never thought of before;
- Thinking about reasons why things are the way they are;
- Looking at things from a different point of view;
- Step by step like a ladder;
- Like a metaphor - working out meaning;
- Having empathy - maybe challenging others' ideas.

Philosophy for Children can develop **skills** of:

- Investigation - by asking relevant questions.
- Evaluation - by the ability to debate issues of significance.
- Analysis - by exercising critical and appreciative judgement in order to distinguish between opinion and fact, belief, prejudice and superstition.
- Application - by making associations between ideas.
- Reflection - by developing the ability to think reflectively about feelings, relationships, experience, ultimate questions, beliefs and practices.
- Empathy - by developing the ability to see the world through the eyes of others, and to see issues from their point of view.
- Expression - by developing the ability to give an informed opinion and express a personal viewpoint.

Philosophy for Children can develop **attitudes** of:

Fairness

- Listening to the views of others without pre-judging;
- Careful consideration of other views;
- Willingness to consider evidence and argument;
- Readiness to look beyond surface impressions.

Respect

- Respecting those who have different beliefs and customs to one's own;
- Recognising the rights of others to hold their views;
- Recognising the needs and concerns of others.

Self-understanding

- Developing a sense of self-worth;
- Developing the capacity to consider one's own beliefs, values and attitudes;
- Understanding and sharing one's own experience of awe and wonder;
- The desire to enter into a personal search for the meaning of life.

Enquiry

- Developing a personal interest in puzzling, searching and challenging questions.
- Developing a responsible and enquiring approach to life generally and in particular to the fundamental questions which it presents.
- Being prepared to acknowledge bias and prejudice in oneself.

These skills and attitudes are just as valid at 3 years old as 90 years old.

'We reinforce our capacity most naturally to remember anything by talking about it as we are doing it.'

Colin Hannaford in 'Teaching the Socrates Way'.

These figures represent the capacity of the average child to retain knowledge after different kinds of class activity:

Listening	5%
Reading	10%
Audio-visual	20%
Demonstrations	30%
Discussion	50%
Practice by doing	75%
Explaining to others	90%

National Literacy Trust; London

Many consider the first three tasks the most effective for teaching and learning, but these are up to twenty times less effective than the last three!

There are, of course, huge issues about the way children are living in the 21st century. In 'Toxic Childhood' (2006) and 'Detoxing Childhood' (2007) Sue Palmer explores the realities of many children's experiences in major areas of their lives, such as food, sleep, family care, pressure at school, consumerism, televisions in bedrooms, outdoor play, exercise, manners and family break-up. These issues themselves would be good topics for children to discuss - philosophically!

Section Two
Philosophy for Children
How to do it

Incorporating P4C in your daily work

This section is about encouraging a thinking attitude to learning in your setting or classroom. If you accept that an enquiring mind is the best mind for learning, then we all need to use philosophy strategies as often as possible, building them in every activity, not just during special sessions. This will mean asking more open-ended questions and giving children much more time to think about answers.

Of course, some areas of learning, some activities and some subjects naturally lend themselves to questioning, debate and enquiry. Personal and Social Development, problem solving, scientific enquiry, and talking about a sense of time, a sense of place and a sense of community all involve us quite naturally in thinking skills such as asking questions and seeking information. Other subjects and aspects may need more planning, and a re-think of the way we work with children to ensure that they are thinking and not just going through activities because we have planned them.

You could:

- Create mind maps (visual pictures made during brainstorming) at the beginning of a new project or unit of work. These can also be used during a project or topic to recap on learning, raise and answer questions and check coverage. Topic sessions in RE, science, history and geography (and their associated areas of learning in the early years) particularly benefit from this technique.

- Use circle times, assemblies and other discussion sessions where children can speak freely to resolve issues, to explore personal, social, emotional, health and citizenship development. Class or whole school assemblies are also great opportunities for thinking and reflection not just being entertained from the front.

- A diary or personal thoughts book for each child gives opportunities for writing and drawing which is personal to the individual child. A group or class thinking diary can also be used for individual and group thoughts, scribed by an adult or a child: this gives an outlet other than speech for questions to be asked and views aired.

Following Children's Own Agendas

Some children would like the 'show and tell' times in school to be just about themselves, as they have so much to share and need someone to listen. It is important for their peace of mind and their emotional security to make as many opportunities to listen and share as possible, either one-to-one with an adult, in small groups or with the whole group. These are times for open-ended questions: How did this make you feel? Why do you think it happened like this?

Most children are inquisitive and desperate to have 'hands on' experience of everything they see, and if they don't want to touch, smell, taste, look and listen we are alarmed. These senses are vital learning tools for every child and they are pre-programmed to use them. Children must be allowed to do just that, and use all their senses to support their learning. Learning is always more effective if more than one sense is used.

In philosophy sessions children are actively encouraged to do this and discuss what they are doing to extend sensory learning. Touching a puzzling object is particularly satisfying - fingers and hands are always ready to help the information being gathered by eyes and ears.

Through philosophy sessions children can also explore current interest in films, TV programmes, books and comics. They can share ideas about the fun and value of keeping fit through swimming lessons, football and dance classes, social times like playing out and visiting friends, the book bus visiting and forthcoming school events such as 'The Big Draw' (where the whole nation is encouraged by Quentin Blake the artist, to run drawing events for adults and children).

All these events in the lives of the children in your care need time for reflection, and ideally for sharing with someone else. Your setting or school may be the only place where some children have the time, the space and the approval to do this.

Interactive Displays about Thinking

Our Philosophy Wall or Thinking Wall

This can be a permanent space where children and adults can display drawings and writing about good ideas, interesting experiences or questions they would like to share. Having a display place which is completely their own can give children a sense of importance, create a reason for writing and give an insight for everyone into what they are thinking and doing. 'Our Philosophy Wall', 'A Space for Thinking' or 'Ideas and Thoughts' might be good titles, but it would be good to ask the children what they think. Add a big sheet of paper and pens nearby for 'ideas in passing.'

A 'Think About' Table

An interactive 'Think About' area is a super way to encourage children to continue interaction with ideas and discussions with friends.

Think about collections (stored in see-through boxes) can contain interesting Artefact which are used not only for 'starters' in philosophy sessions but for continued interaction. These can be placed at strategic places in halls and corridors, where queues form and in every class room. Their contents will vary depending on the topic but they are fun to create and can be shared with other groups throughout the school who may add ideas and Artefact.

Things to collect for interesting, interactive displays are:

- laminated greetings cards and photos;
- lengths of interesting fabrics from different cultures and countries;
- Artefact;
- laminated words and labels, which explain the display are a flexible resource for adults and children (headings, titles, labels, arrows, names etc);
- some philosophical questions on cards to encourage thinking;
- notepads, clip boards, pens, pencils for children to add their own writing and drawings;
- picture books, fiction and non-fiction;
- space for pictures, models or findings created during the sessions;
- cameras, tape recorders, dictaphones, Talking Tins;
  - role play clothing and equipment nearby would encourage play on the theme too.

If the children are part of the process of constructing these displays, they will be much more interested in them, and will take much more care of the objects on display. Children have their own ideas about displays and we should let them try these out, even if they don't fit with ours! Where space is at a premium even the seat of a chair can be used for an adequate display but it is very useful if there is room all around the display for people to meet to have thoughts and discussions! Seating nearby may also be useful.

Some **ideas for collections** and **starter questions** are:

Animals - Why are there so many different animals in the world?

Buildings - Do we need buildings?

Colour - How do different colours make you feel?

Fabric - When you look at different fabrics, what do they remind you of?

Flowers - What are flowers for?

Leaves - How many different sorts and shapes of leaves do you think there are?

Machines - Can humans do things that machines can't?

Maps - Could anyone go to every place in the world?

Metal - Is metal more valuable than plastic? Where does metal come from?

Mini beasts - What do minibeasts do? Could we live without them?

Space - What is it like in outer space?

Pattern - What are patterns for?

Picture books - How can a picture tell a story?

Plants - Why are there different plants in different countries?

Plastic - How is plastic made? Why do we need it?

Poetry books - Why do people write and read poetry?

Pottery - How does clay turn into hard pottery?

Sand - What does sand feel like? Where does it come from?

Seasons - Autumn, Winter, Spring, Summer - What are the signs of different seasons?

Shells - Why do we hear the ocean inside a shell?

Shiny things - Why do we love shiny things?

Toys - Why do we need toys? Could we manage without them?

Water - Why do we need water in our world?

Wood - Will all the trees in the world ever get used up?

Give us time to think about the important and difficult questions.

In the middle of a corridor display of 10 picture postcards with a wide variety of subjects was the following question:

Which picture do you find most interesting and why?

Children voted by writing comments and recording a vote on a clipboard as they went to and from lunch or round the school. After 2 to 3 weeks the voting was recorded:

Most people liked the stones laid in a pattern in shallow water.

(this was a natural sculpture by Andy Goldsworthy)

Someone wrote 'How did this happen?'
Someone else wrote: 'Because it is different from most things, and it's in the ocean.'

Another interactive corridor display of night time pictures asked the question:

'When out at night wear white.' - Why?

Children's comments included:

'So cars can see you.'

'To be seen.'

'So you look cool.'

'Because people can see you more.'

'In case somebody has died and their (they're) in a coffin because white shows respect.'

'So the cars on the street can see you and nothing will happen.'

'You wear bright clothes at night so people can see you.'

'So God can see you are wearing white.'

'It is a nice colour.'

'Because if you wear white nothing will happen to you.'

'If you cross the road cars can see that you are crossing.'

'So you can be seen.'

'So an accident won't happen to you.'

'So you shine bright.'

Don't just DO something - STAND there!

'Listening to lots of different views rather than just one means you can decide for yourself, instead of just being told what to think.
Don't you agree? You don't have to of course.'

The Guardian 2007

'Think About' boxes and collections to explore

A 'Think About People' box might contain:

- Dorling Kindersley books 'Celebrations!'and 'Children Just Like Me' Barnabas and Ana Kindersley;
- models and figures made from different media e.g. soapstone family, Lego or Playmobil people, pipe cleaners, peg figures or people puppets;
- pictures and photos of people of all ages, cultures, backgrounds, laminated or on post cards, from magazines and catalogues, class photos;
- fabric with printed or embroidered human figures;
- a role play box with clothing from all sorts of cultures and countries.

Some philosophical questions:

- What would the world be like with no people?
- Are any people the same?
- How can people live in harmony?
- What is a family?
- What does 'old' mean? When do you start being old?
- What would happen if no more babies were born?
- Why do people choose to live in different countries?

A 'Think About Wood' box might contain:

- appropriate coloured fabrics for drapes - different browns and greens, bark and leaf patterns;
- postcard-sized, laminated pictures of forests, trees, wooden objects;
- different pieces of wood, bark, a log with growth rings, wood slices, roots, twigs and branches, driftwood;
- wooden objects - carvings, household objects such as wooden spoons, bowls, wooden beads and jewellery;
- leaves of all sorts;
- seeds from trees - acorns, conkers, cones, a sprouting conker or acorn;
- a wooden log and nails with hammer to knock them in;
- books about trees - non-fiction and stories such as Percy the Park Keeper;
- a role play box with park keepers gear or Robin Hood clothing.

Philosophical questions:
- Why do we need trees in our world?
- How would human beings survive without trees and wood?
- Where did the first trees come from?
- Will all the trees in the world ever get used up?

Clive Bell (philosopher 1881-1964)

'Only reason can convince us of those three fundamental truths without a recognition of which there can be no effective liberty:

that what we believe is not necessarily true;
that what we like is not necessarily good;
and that all questions are open.'

27

Mini-P4C sessions - simple ideas which encourage group reflection

These games allow children to
- show control
- show collaboration and team work
- respond to peer pressure
- have a shared focus
- work as a member of a group

'How in the World?' calendar game

Use a calendar with nature scenes - cut out the pictures and display them round the room; ask the children to talk to each other about the scenes and write or suggest captions for the pictures.

One potato, two potato

Give each child a potato to hold:
- look at it;
- feel its shape;
- look for any bumps;
- look for individual markings;
- look at its colour and the texture of its skin;
- then return the potatoes to a bag.

Tip the potatoes back out on display and ask the children to find their own potato. Discuss how they knew which one was theirs.

This could be done with other vegetables or fruit, pebbles, shells or conkers - anything which is fairly similar.

One child, two children

Remember the potato game?

How can we tell we are each different (especially if we are in school uniform)?

Myself, my place

Draw a picture about your favourite place and tell people why it is your favourite place - put it in a display frame.

Chaos

At circle time - place lots of balls on the floor - ask a child to find a way to pick them all up at once - they will find this difficult or impossible! Think together about how it could be done, possibly with several people working together - reflect on how well the job was done then.

Everybody up

Everyone sitting on chairs in a circle. Children stand up one at a time: if they stand when another does they both have to sit down and stay sitting. This encourages the group to be aware of each other and to be less self centred. Find time to ask how everyone felt about this game.

Design together

Each child draws a line on a large sheet of paper, one at a time. It is interesting to see each child's personality revealed in this exercise: some try for the original swirl others make insignificant-looking squiggles. Talk about the picture.

Pass the parcel

Pass a piece of paper, a box of Smarties, a pair of scissors, a bunch of keys or a tambourine round the circle without making a sound.

Editing

Pass an object around (this denotes your turn) with a person standing in the middle listening to what everyone says their favourite fruit/TV programme/music/colour/food. The person in the middle then reports the common themes of what everyone said - for example, 'Most people like bananas best' or 'Everyone said something different' or 'Everyone copied what their friend said' or 'No-one chose my favourite'.

Sometimes children really like to think about BIG questions such as:

What would happen if all the animals disappeared from the world?

What would happen if all the plants disappeared from the world?

What would happen if all the water disappeared from the world?

What would happen if the sunshine disappeared from the world?

What would happen if children could fly?

What would happen if Lego stuck for ever?

What would happen if there were no mirrors?

What would happen if everyone had the same name?

What would happen if all the cups disappeared?

What would happen if there were no knives?

What would happen if escalators only went up?

What would happen if books had no pictures?

What would happen if cars went backwards?

What would happen if there were no guns?

What would happen if bubbles didn't pop?

What would happen if there were no schools?

What would happen if there was no more TV?

What would happen if we all wore glasses?

What would happen if milk was green?

What would happen if we all forgot how to walk?

What would happen if fish could sing?

What would happen if you could play outside all day?

What would happen if there were no more babies?

What would happen if children were big and grown ups were small?

What would happen if all jigsaws had the same picture?

What would happen if it never rained again?

What would happen if ants were as big as mice?

Philosophy for children out of doors

There is so much to look at, feel and experience out of doors, so you can easily incorporate outdoor activities and discussions in your plans for P4C conversations, both in more structured sessions and informally.

Organise your day and week so you can take advantage of good weather to hold sessions outside whenever the weather allows - heavy rain or strong wind make conversations difficult, but on calmer, even dull days, the peace and quiet will be a a positive asset to thinking and contemplation.

The outdoor environment itself can provide many topics for enquiry:

- Why do we like playing outside?
- What do you think of when you look at the sky?
- Why is the sky blue? Is the sky still blue above the clouds?
- Why do we need rain, sun, wind, snow? What makes it happen?
- Why don't we have enough bikes for everyone to have one?
- Why do we have to share the building bricks?
- What makes plants, trees, flowers grow? Why are they there?
- What makes vandals spoil our garden or play area?
- How do shadows happen?

Other ways to use the outdoors are going for a 'walk of awareness', a 'collection walk' or a 'listening walk' at regular intervals to see how the environment changes through the seasons, different times of day and in different weather, to take photos and to collect objects for discussion. Neighbourhood walks allow the children to talk about things they have done with their family and friends in their special local places.

'Draw things you hear on your walk; find something that smells; find something smooth; find something rough; work with a partner to...'

'How do you feel after your walk?' 'Why do you feel this way?' 'Share your feelings with a partner.'

'Run fast for a long time in a large space... how does this make you feel?'

These are some of the responses of very young children to being out of doors exploring the garden of their setting or school:

In the KS1 playground

'You can follow the lines, play on circles, go round the circles, follow the (giant) pencils in a game, run twirly-whirly till you get to the middle, swap lines and play hopscotch; it's boring without toys, it's not nice when there's nothing to play with. You could do racing and it's useful to have pencils, throwing the ball into the middle - if we didn't have circle couldn't do it, you can pretend, but not as nice.'

Of the Adventure Trail

'It's so nice to play on the field and good fun to play 'Tig off ground' and 'Tig-bob-down'. We can learn: climbing, hopping, balancing, racing, falling, rolling, jumping, crawling, running, chasing, 1 leg balancing.'

In the Community garden

'It looks nice; it's pretty beautiful.'

At the Public Library

'You can get a book - help us to read; learn things so we'll be good at writing, learn about computers.'

Why are there flowers in the world? (sitting in school garden)

'To make stuff look pretty, to smell nice, when its spring daffodils come out, if you pick them they die but they come back, looks good in school, to look at and smell.'

Why we need water? (sitting near the brook in the school grounds)

'So your mouth doesn't go dry when you talk, for jelly, for flowers, for washing up, to iron, to help us grow, to sweat, for ducks and for plants, for crying, its healthy to drink, to flush the toilet, to play with in the water tray, to wash hands, for bathing, for brushing your teeth, shells need it, fish need it, for swimming, to wash clothes, for painting, for drinking.'

Thinking about trees (having hugged some tree trunks, now sitting underneath one):

'It's an old tree because it bends.'

'The tree feels very rough.'

'You can make wooden toys.'

'The tree is green and brown.'

'All the branches are different.'

'You can get apples from trees.'

'You can get flowers form trees.'

'If there were no trees there would be no apples.'

'All trees are different when they are babies and then they grown and grow.'

'Some have flowers on and some don't.'

'Trees are spiky.'

'If you pull off the bark they go orange.'

'The leaves are smooth but rough at the back.'

'They fall and die then new ones come.'

'Trees have roots and go all in the ground.'

'Some trees are high.'

'You can make a tree house.'

'Monkeys play in trees.'

'We went shopping and saw a tree being chopped down.'

'When the tee falls down it will die.'

'Put lots of seeds in the ground and put soil over it then trees will grow.'

'Plant pear seeds they will grow.'

Why do we need trees? (a discussion out of doors):

'They're fun to climb.'

'Get fruit from.'

'Giraffes need them to eat the leaves.'

'Caterpillars need to eat them.'

'Squint if didn't have shade from them.'

'For birds to sit in.'

'For squirrels to find food.'

'Twigs for birds to make a nest.'

'Nuts come from trees.'

'Flowers to make air freshener with.'

'To get wood from.'

'For bees to live in.'

'Why do some plants smell nice, some smell nasty and some don't smell at all?'

Everything out of doors can inspire questions to ask and answer, from litter and pollution to cloud formations, from mini beasts under a log to buddleia growing on the roof, from dinner play problems to sharing 'the best bike'. Take the thinking out of doors!

Using Action Songs and Movement Exercises for P4C

These are great for drawing the group together or for a break in deliberations and recharging the brain for thinking:

Familiar favourites are the easiest to remember. Here are some favourites:
- A Sailor Went to Sea, Sea, Sea - to see what he could see, see, see. But all that he could see, see, see was the bottom of the deep blue sea, sea, sea.
- Heads, Shoulders, Knees and Toes, Knees and Toes
- Ring a Ring of Roses
- There Was a Princess Long Ago
- If You're Happy and You Know it Clap Your Hands - stamp your feet/nod your head/wiggle your hips/bend your knees
- In and Out the Windows
- Oh, the Grand Old Duke of York
- Put Your Finger on Your Head - on your head/on your chest/behind your back/under your chin etc
- There's a Brown Girl in the Ring - she looks like the sugar in a plum
- Here We Go Looby Lou - put your right arm in/left leg in etc.
- Here We Go Round the Mulberry Bush
- She'll Be Coming Round the Mountain When She Comes
- Little Peter Rabbit has a Fly Upon his Nose
- In a Cottage in a Wood

Echo songs and action games can keep everyone alert and responsive and the tune can be made up as you go along!

- I'm ready - are you? (I'm ready - are you?)
- Oops I need to tie my shoe! (Echo)

- Now I'm ready to tap my toes (Echo)
- Oops I need to blow my nose! (Echo)

- Now I'm ready to sit down (Echo)
- Oh dear, how I frown (Echo)

- Let's sit quietly on a chair (Echo)
- No-one will know we are sitting there (Echo)

- I am ready to hear you speak (Echo)
- I've been waiting about a week! (Echo)

Drums and beaters provide a good rhythm for marching or dancing.

A bird whistle or Swannee Whistle (with a moveable 'tongue') is great for encouraging the group to stand - slowly up, then quickly down etc.

Listening to music is a useful way to draw the group together. Calm music often stills the atmosphere and if the facilitator shows that they are engrossed in listening to the music then the group is assured about what is expected. Most music by Karl Jenkins is suitable for listening to in this way: it has a joyous quality yet begs to be listened to not 'talked over!' It can also be used to move to sitting down with arms and hands: this collective music and movement is a great group empathy-builder.

Clapping Games by Jenny Mosley ISBN 0-954058542 has a Big Book and CD to sing along with e.g. 'Clap Out, Clap In' and 'I-diddle-I Clap up High'.

This Little Puffin by Elizabeth Matterson ISBN 0-14-034048-3 is a great resource to have nearby - almost any page will be suitable!

A Nursery Rhymes tape to sing along with is useful, especially if you dance at the same time. Try Carousel Nursery Rhymes, available from Featherstone Education

Music Express by Sue Nichols, Patricia Scott and Sally Hickman ISBN 0713665823 has some great action songs and a lively CD with songs such as 'One Wobbly Bicycle Went Riding Round the Town,' and 'Hands High, Look at Me, To the Sky, Look at Me'.

Section Three
Planning P4C Sessions

The shape of a Philosophy for Children session

Clear rules are essential:

- **One person speaks at a time**

  '**OOPSAaT**' - only one person speaks at a time - is a fun way to remind them.

- **We all look at and listen to the speaker**
- **We indicate when we wish to speak with an agreed sign**
- **We give a reason for our views**
- **We are kind to each other even when we don't agree.**

Consider how you will decide on the rules. You could use these simple ones to begin with and change them as time goes on and the children want to make up their own. Your help at the beginning will ensure the success of the process - remember, the children won't know what P4C is until you start!

Sitting in a circle gives a strong sense of being in a group, with no-one more important that anyone else. This also gives a central focus and easy view for the stimulus you have chosen to use. The only exception to the circle may be when you use a picture book, when a group gathered together makes it easier for everyone to see the illustrations.

Adults MUST model the behaviour they wish the children to follow.

Some words of wisdom

- No-one is without knowledge except him who asks no questions - Fulfulde, Gambia
- You cannot tell the contents of the parcel until you open it - Ugandan proverb
- Asking questions will enable you to find the right answer - Mende, Sierra Leone
- It is through other people's wisdom that we learn wisdom: a single person's understanding does not amount to anything - Yoruba, Nigeria
- It is better to build bridges than walls - Swahili, Kenya

From '**Wit and Wisdom of Africa**' Patrick Ibekwe

The Ten Elements

Each P4C session has ten elements:

1. Preparation (seating, establishing calm)

Keep the group as small as possible - under 12 is ideal. You could have the whole class involved in a philosophy session together, but this is obviously going to limit individual contributions, and as the EYFS recommends that all discussion in the early years should be in smaller groups, we should all be trying to arrange this wherever possible. It is also vital at this point to establish or remind children of the **speaking and listening rules** for the group, which may include:

- Only one person speaks at a time ('OOPSAaT');
- We all look at the person who is speaking;
- We give a reason for our opinions;
- When we want to speak, we make the agreed sign (an arm across the chest, a hand on the knee, or another sign the group chooses. Avoid arm-waving, it is distracting in a group and tiring if you are waiting a long time);
- We are kind to each other even when we don't agree.

A P4C Session - Stages 1-10

2. **Presentation** (the stimulus)

This can be odd-one-out activity, a story, some pictures, a piece of music, an artefact, poetry or a persona doll. It is useful to establish a routine with one sort of stimulus (such as a picture) before moving on to a different sort. This embeds the routine before you move on to another kind of stimulus.

3. Thinking time (time to reflect quietly on the stimulus)

A short space for thinking is valuable for children, giving peace and quiet to get their thoughts collected and to observe the stimulus you are offering.

4. **Conversation** (in twos and threes)

Conversations with one other child (a 'knee-' or 'elbow-buddy') to try out ideas and contributions, are much less intimidating than speaking to the whole group.

5. Formulation (thinking of and sharing questions)

This is a skilled, time-consuming activity. You will need to give plenty of time, particularly when children are unfamiliar with the process, but after several philosophy sessions it will become embedded in your routine. Writing the questions down is useful at this stage (and the questioner's name if you need a memory prompt!). You could use a flip chart or whiteboard for recording the questions so all the children can see them.

6. Airing (thinking about the questions)

Children now need time to look at and reflect on the suggested questions, and you may need to remind everyone of what has been suggested and think about whether it is a suitable philosophical or thinking question. '**How many toys has the boy got in the picture?**' is not a suitable question because they could easily be counted without much thinking, but '**WHY has the boy got so many toys?**' would be a good question as it requires a reasoned answer.

7. Selection (voting on the order of the discussion)

As you begin, you may need to re-read the questions as the children think and select their preferred ones. When the children get more familiar with the process, thinking of questions for discussion will become second nature, and the value of the democratic voting to find 'THE' starting question will become an essential part of the process. When children start to experience philosophy sessions voting may not be appropriate. As you incorporate this in your sessions, it is useful for young children to use a token to vote with - a shiny button or a pebble to put in a container helps to avoid enthusiastic over-voting.

It is also useful here before the discussion starts to do a **short physical exercise**, such as an action song or circle dance to loosen up any stiffness and to ensure everyone is alert.

8. First words

As the discussion starts the children may be slow to respond but be patient and eventually the debate will flow. The role of the facilitator is to ensure that people waiting to talk have a turn, and at this point there will be some brilliant ideas and some ordinary ones - respond to each equally. The great value of these sessions is that every child should feel they are contributing to the whole discussion; there are no right or wrong answers and all their opinions are valid.

9. Building and developing the thinking (being critical and creative)

This is the core of the process, and should be a time when everyone is thinking, listening and concentrating, particularly when philosophy sessions are well-embedded in the group. Ideas flow backwards and forwards, people change their minds, become entrenched in their views or stun others with their insight! Some children will still be observers and skilled facilitation may be needed to encourage their participation, although the right to silence should always be respected.

10. Last words

The session will eventually have to come to an end and the facilitator should thank everyone for their contributions to an interesting discussion before closing the proceedings with some time for reflection, quiet music or a song.

What makes a good question?

Philosophical questions are those open-ended ones which allow for a range of answers, of views to be expressed and a debate to be enjoyed. They encourage children to talk about their own ideas because they are thinking their own thoughts, not deciding what **you** want them to think is the correct answer to a question! They don't need to rely on evidence, statistics or data which might not be known or remembered, and they often address the big questions of life.

Can you ask a question that has no answer?

Some of the questions children ask:

Why does the sun come up?

Where is the sun when we can't see it?

Where do people (or pets) go when they die?

Who is God?

Why do bad things happen?

What is a rainbow?

What is a dream?

Why do people snore?

What would happen if you didn't drink anything?

Why is the moon there on some nights and not on others?

How do lambs know which sheep is their mum?

Are all stories true?

What makes flowers smell?

How does the Internet work?

Can you ask a question about something you know nothing about?

and some you may devise together:

How could you make someone happy?

Can you lie without meaning to do so?

How do we know if something is true?

Where were we before we were born?

Why do we all look different?

How did that make you feel?

What does honest mean?

How could you stop a baby crying?

Is there such a thing as the real truth?

Where is a thing when we can't see it?

How do we learn to do things?

What is the same about all of us?

Who tells you what to do?

Can you tell a little lie?

How is... feeling?

What do you think... is wondering?

What might this person do next/decide?

How would you feel if...?

What is the meaning of... ?

Can you think of another meaning for?

Why do you think... do, say, believe that?

What is colour?

What is in space?

What is perfume?

What is the difference between thinking and dreaming?

How could we make the world a better place?

What did this picture/story make you think about?

How could the story end differently?

Are humans the only beings with minds?

Can you touch your mind?

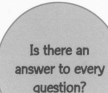

Is there an answer to every question?

What makes us think?

Where do thoughts come from?

Can you name something that...?

Why do some things make you happy and some things make you sad?

How is this similar to... different from?

Can you explain what must have happened?

What do you think happened before that?

What is the key moment in the story?

Why do you say this?

Where is your heart?

Can your heart talk to your brain?

Can it be good to get angry?

What is important enough to get angry about?

Section Four
Examples of Planned Sessions

Examples of Planned Sessions
Odd one out

When children first begin to get involved in thinking philosophically, it's important to encourage every child to be involved and contribute to the discussion and shared thinking. This can be scary for some children who are reluctant to speak, naturally quiet, or sometimes overwhelmed in a large group. Working in smaller groups can eliminate some of that fear. Using '**odd one out**' as a starting point means that everyone starts from the same place, a very inclusive way to begin.

Children unused to being asked about their ideas may be slow to start speaking independently when they first try. Using '**odd one out**' they can see how agreeing with others is an easy way to gain the confidence to speak your mind.

'**Odd one out**' is also the easiest of activities to set up because it really can be three objects grabbed from a shelf - there is no need to think whether they are the same or different when you choose them!

What you need: 3 real objects to handle, such as

- a wooden bowl, a wooden spoon and a twig
- an orange, a conker and a bowl of dried beans
- three different sorts of flowers or leaves
- a shell, a stone and a brick

What you say: 'Let's find the odd one out'.

What the children might say:

'I think the wooden bowl is the odd one out because you can mix things in it but you can't mix things inside a twig or a wooden spoon.'

Each child has a chance to say what they think. Encourage them by your open response and supportive comments.

'I think the red flower is the odd one out because it has lots of petals and the other two have just a few petals.'

Odd one out activities need lots of practice in thinking of, and adding reasons for, your sentence and not just repeating what someone else has said or giving one word answers.

Title: Odd one out - thinking about same and different
Group size: up to 12 children
Time: 15-20 minutes

Learning intention:
To encourage and develop thinking and speaking skills using three objects for stimulus, and to work cooperatively in a group.

Possible learning outcomes:
Children will be comfortable with thinking before they speak and keen to listen to other people's opinions and engage in discussion.
They will take turns to speak and use appropriate listening body language.

Resources:
Essential:
3 different objects - they can be anything:
  - a plant in a pot, a pear, a box of dominoes
  - a wooden box, a plastic spoon, some patterned wrapping paper
  - a candle, a piece of ribbon, a bag of flour

A copy of the 'speaking in philosophy time' **rules**
  - only one person speaks at a time
  - use the special signal to show you wish to speak (a hand across your body, a hand resting on your shoulder, a finger on your chin)
  - look at the person who is speaking
  - try to give a reason for your opinion
  - sit together in a circle.

Specific vocabulary	
odd-one-out	opinion
same/different	reflection
views	calm
opinions	quiet
study	choose
philosophy	question
speaking	open-ended
thinking	different
listening	similar
responding	like
ideas	unlike
agree	objects
disagree	

Overview of the session:

The children look at the 3 objects and talk about their differences and similarities; they take turns to speak, according to the group rules, sharing their ideas with respect for others' opinions.

Main activity:

Welcome children to the philosophy or thinking circle.

Remind them of the rules for discussion, recapping on why you have them.

Explain that you have three objects to show them, and for them to think about.

Place the objects on the floor in the centre of the group and say:

'We are going to think about which object might be the odd one out and why we think that'.

Allow plenty of thinking time for children to formulate their ideas, and signal that they wish to speak. It is rare that no-one wants to speak, but it doesn't matter if there is a lull, the ideas will eventually flow.

Extension activity:

Extend the session to allow more time for discussion, or add more objects.

Plenary:

Ask what the children found interesting about the session. Thank them for all their thinking, sharing and good ideas. Talk about how well they cooperated and listened, and how they showed their thinking skills.

Differentiation:

Less able: Encourage them to contribute by initially asking them whose idea they agree with; always look directly at individuals to encourage participation. Praise all contributions.

More able: Philosophical thinking allows the more-able to push their minds to the limits - allow them to do that by encouraging thinking 'outside the box'.

Profile references:	Cross-curricular links for Foundation Stage:
LCT 1, 2, 3, and 5, 6, 7, 8, 9	DA 1, 6, 8 SD 2, 3, 5, 6, 7, 9
KS1 Core literacy: all those listed except those which specifically refer to 'text'.	ED 3, 5, 7, 8, 9
	KUW 5
	CD 7
	KS1 - all topics

Title: Thinking about painting
Group size: up to 12 children
Time: 15-20 minutes

Learning intention:

To encourage and develop thinking and speaking skills using an art work as stimulus and to work cooperatively in the group.

Possible learning outcomes:

Children will become more used to thinking before they speak and are keen to listen to other people's opinions and engage in discussion.

They will become used to taking turns to speak and use appropriate listening body language.

Resources:

Essential:

A poster of a large painting such as:

- Wassily Kandinsky 'Cossacks'
- Pieter Bruegel 'Peasant Wedding Feast' or
- Georges Seurat 'Sunday afternoon on the Grande Jatte'

covered with a large piece of plain paper that has hinged flaps so that you can reveal small parts of the picture at a time.

You also need a copy of the 'speaking in philosophy time' rules

Overview of the session:

Children share their responses to seeing part of the picture before sharing in the revealing of and responding to the whole picture.

Specific vocabulary	
art	responding
painting	ideas
artists	agree
oil	disagree
watercolours	opinion
frames	reflection
gallery	calm
work of art	quiet
picture	choose
philosophy	question
speaking	open-ended
thinking	
listening	

Main activity:

Welcome children to the philosophy or thinking circle.

Remind them of the rules for discussion, recapping on why you have these rules.

Explain that you have a painting which has been covered up, so you can only look at a tiny piece at a time. Lift one flap and ask the children to talk about what they can see and what they think the 'big picture' is. Keep opening flaps and talking about the painting as ideas shift and more of it is revealed. When all these ideas have been exhausted look at the whole painting together. Encourage the children to talk about their reactions when they view it. Did they see anything new?

Extension activity:

Had anyone got close to the true picture with their ideas?

Does it matter whether they guessed rightly or wrongly?

Plenary:

Ask the children what they found interesting about the session. Thank them for their thinking, sharing and good ideas. Comment on how well they cooperated and listened and how what they said showed their thinking skills.

Additional resources and enrichment:

Use the interactive whiteboard to use art work in this way with hide and reveal buttons (e.g. Promethean Active Primary software).

Profile references:	Cross-curricular links for Foundation Stage:
LCT 1, 2, 3, and 5, 6, 7, 8, 9	DA 1, 6, 8
KS1 Core literacy: all those listed except those which specifically refer to 'text'.	SD 2, 3, 5, 6, 7, 9
	ED 3, 5, 7, 8, 9
	KUW 5 CD 7
	KS1 - all topics

Title: **Thinking about drawings and photos**

Group size: **up to 12 children**

Time: **15-20 minutes**

Learning intentions:

To encourage and develop thinking and speaking skills using picture cards a stimulus for ideas and to work cooperatively in the group. Taking turns to speak and use appropriate listening body language.

Possible learning outcomes:

Children will become more comfortable with thinking before they speak, will be keen to listen to other people's opinions and engage in discussion.

Resources:

Essential:

Christmas, birthday cards, postcards or photos for children to study and sort into categories: about 20-30 cards for this size of group would be enough.

A copy of the 'speaking in philosophy time' **rules**

- only one person speaks at a time
- use the special signal to show you wish to speak (a hand across your body, a hand resting on your shoulder, a finger on your chin)
- look at the person who is speaking
- try to give a reason for your opinion
- sit together in a circle.

Overview of the session:

Children work in small groups to sort and categorise picture cards. They share their thinking and reasoning with the other groups.

Specific vocabulary

picture	ideas
similar	agree
different	disagree
colourful	opinion
patterned	reflection
photo	calm
painting	quiet
cards	choose
philosophy	question
speaking	open-ended
thinking	
listening	
responding	

Main activity:

Welcome children to the philosophy or thinking circle.

Remind them of the rules for discussion, recapping on why you have these rules.

Ask the children to get into groups of 3 or 4 on the carpet and share the cards between them on the floor.

The groups can then look at the cards, talk to each other about them and sort them into groups which they can explain to the other groups - they might sort Christmas cards with all the holly berry cards together, all cards with red on, cards with shepherds on. When the groups are ready, they share their findings, saying why they have chosen to sort the way they have.

Extension activity:

Mix the groups and re-deal the cards to reinforce respectful, shared discussion and widen the variety of criteria for sorting.

Plenary:

Ask what they found interesting about the session - 'Could you have done this activity without speaking?' 'How many ways could you find for sorting the cards if you had more time?'

Praise the children for their thinking, sharing and good ideas. Comment positively on how well they cooperated and listened and how what they said showed their thinking skills.

Additional resources and enrichment:

Lots of laminated picture cards - it's worth building up a wide variety for your collection as they have lots of potential for   philosophical enquiry sessions and general discussion.

Profile references:	Cross-curricular links for Foundation Stage:
LCT 1, 2, 3, and 5, 6, 7, 8, 9	DA 1, 6, 8
KS1 Core literacy: all those listed except those which specifically refer to 'text'.	SD 2, 3, 5, 6, 7, 9
	ED 3, 5, 7, 8, 9
	KUW 5
	CD 7
	KS1 - all topics

Title: Thinking about Artefacts
Group size: up to 12 children
Time: 15-20 minutes

Learning intention:

To encourage and develop thinking and speaking skills using Artefact for stimulus; to work cooperatively in the group.

Possible learning outcomes:

Children become more comfortable with thinking before they speak and more able to listen to other people's opinions and engage in discussion.

Resources:

Essential:

A special artefact - try to find one with a specific purpose - huge wind chimes from Bali; a large marimba (wooden xylophone) from Africa; a decorated mask; a souvenir from your last holiday; a photo of one of Andy Goldsworthy's sculptures or an abstract sculpture.

A copy of the 'speaking in philosophy time' rules

- only one person speaks at a time
- use the special signal to show you wish to speak (a hand across your body, a hand resting on your shoulder, a finger on your chin)
- look at the person who is speaking
- try to give a reason for your opinion
- sit together in a circle.

Overview of the session:

Children examine the special artefact, discuss what it might be made from, or used for, and why the artist made it.

Specific vocabulary

artefact	philosophy
sculpture	speaking
art work	thinking
ornament	listen/respond
craft work	ideas
ceramic	agree
bronze	disagree opinion
wood	reflection
created	clam
made	quiet
artist	choose
sculpture	question
pattern-maker	open-ended

Main activity:

Welcome children to the philosophy or thinking circle. Remind them of the rules for discussion, recapping on why you have these.

Explain that you are going to look at a special artefact and discuss what it might be used for and why the artist made it. Pass the object round or move in to touch it one by one if it is too large to move.

After some thinking time, ask the question again. If you wish you can list the children's suggestions on the whiteboard or a flip chart, adding the reasons WHY they think what they do. Talk about the range of ideas. Look at the similarities and differences in the suggestions, agreement and disagreement and how this can be resolved 'I think I understand your point of view but I don't agree with you because...'

Extension activity:

Ask 'WHY do people make things like this?' 'What are works of art for?'

Plenary:

Talk about how well the children cooperated and listened and how what they said showed how well they are using their thinking skills. Ask what they found interesting about the session. Thank the children for all their thinking, sharing and good ideas.

Enrichment:

Try to find some more exciting Artefact - perhaps you could sit near a dinosaur skeleton in a museum and think and talk about that.

Profile references:	Cross-curricular links for Foundation Stage:
LCT 1, 2, 3, and 5, 6, 7, 8, 9 KS1 Core literacy: all those listed except those which specifically refer to 'text'.	DA 1, 6, 8 SD 2, 3, 5, 6, 7, 9 ED 3, 5, 7, 8, 9 KUW 5 CD 7 KS1 - all topics

Title: Thinking about drawing together
Group size: up to 12 children
Time: 15-20 minutes

Learning intention:

To encourage and develop thinking and speaking skills using collective drawing as stimulus and to work cooperatively in the group. Taking turns to speak and use appropriate listening body language.

Possible learning outcomes:

Children are more comfortable with thinking before they speak, keen to listen to other people's opinions, and engage in discussion.

Resources:

Essential:

A large sheet of paper and large felt pen

Whiteboard/flip chart and pen for writing up ideas

Voting tokens - buttons, shells, pebbles - one per child

A copy of the 'speaking in philosophy time' rules

- only one person speaks at a time
- use the special signal to show you wish to speak (a hand across your body, a hand resting on your shoulder, a finger on your chin)
- look at the person who is speaking
- try to give a reason for your opinion
- sit together in a circle.

Overview of the session:

The children draw a picture together and vote for a title.

Specific vocabulary

drawing	responding
design	ideas
ideas	agree
artist	disagree
sketch	opinion
lines	reflection
swirls/shapes	clam
philosophy	quiet
speaking	choose
thinking	question
listening	open-ended

Main activity:

Welcome children to the philosophy circle and remind them of the rules for discussion, recapping on why you have these rules.

'Today we are going to draw a communal picture, by drawing a line each, one at a time. Then we will look at it and decide what our picture will be called.'

One by one children contribute to the picture. - children's personalities are often revealed here with timid wiggles and large flamboyant streaks!

When everyone has had their turn, look at the drawing together and ask for suggestions for a title, encouraging children to say why they are suggesting and write these down as you go along, ready for the voting. Use tokens for voting so you can make sure everyone votes.

Go through the list of suggestions, one by one, collecting the tokens as people vote. If the suggestions are on a flip chart, tear the paper off and put it on the floor, then everyone can see the votes against the titles and understand the voting better. If there is a tie, have a re-vote with the tied titles.

When a title has been agreed, put it near the painting. Laminating and labelling this picture is a further confirmation of the cooperation that has gone into making it.

Extension activity: Repeat the activity at another time with more paper and assorted pens or paint.

Plenary:

Talk with the children about the good things and difficulties of doing something together. What works and what doesn't?

Ask what it feels like if your suggestion for the title has or hasn't been chosen. How do you feel? Is it fair to vote? This will help them to begin understanding the democratic process.

Thank the children for all their drawing and good ideas for the title. Praise their turn taking and concentration.

Additional resources and enrichment:

More large sheets of paper and assorted large felt pens.

Profile references:	Cross-curricular links for Foundation Stage:
LCT 1, 2, 3, and 5, 6, 7, 8, 9	DA 1, 6, 8 SD 2, 3, 5, 6, 7, 9
KS1 Core literacy: all those listed except those which specifically refer to 'text'.	ED 3, 5, 7, 8, 9 KUW 5
	CD 7, 8 KS1 - all topics

Title: Thinking about music
Group size: up to 12 children
Time: 15-20 minutes

Learning intention:
To encourage and develop thinking and speaking skills using music as a stimulus; to work cooperatively in a group.

Possible learning outcomes:
Children will become more comfortable with thinking before they speak and keen to listen to other people's opinions and engage in discussion. They will become more able to take turns to speak and use appropriate listening body language.

Resources:
Essential:
A piece of music e.g. Karl Jenkins 'Tintinnabulum' and CD player.
Other music suggestions: Saint Saens 'Carnival of the animals'; South American pan pipes music; Indian tabla drums beating.
Whiteboard or flip chart
A copy of the 'speaking in philosophy time' rules
  - only one person speaks at a time
  - use the special signal to show you wish to speak (a hand across your body, a hand resting on your shoulder, a finger on your chin)
  - look at the person who is speaking
  - try to give a reason for your opinion
  - sit together in a circle.

Overview of the session:
Children listen to some music, thinking about the question 'Where do you think you are when you hear this music?' then have an extended discussion about this question, sharing ideas and opinions.

Specific vocabulary

music	thinking
sound	listening
orchestra	responding
instrumentalist	ideas
soloists	agree
classical	disagree
popular	opinion
hear	reflection
like	calm
dislike	quiet
enjoy	choose
feel	question
philosophy	open-ended
speaking	

Main activity:

Welcome children to the philosophy circle. Remind them of the rules for discussion recapping on why you have these rules. Listen to the music while thinking of the question: 'Where do you think you are when you hear this music?' (This particular piece starts off very solemnly and then into joyful singing; you can pause the music to talk about the first part, asking the following question:

'What place does this music remind you of?'

Restart the music and ask the same question again for further discussion. If you wish you can list the different suggestions, always stating WHY they think this on the whiteboard to see how far-ranging children's ideas are. Look at the similarities and differences in people's suggestions. Listen to the music again and continue with the discussion: see whether anyone has changed their minds in the light of other people's suggestions.

Extension activity:

Are there any questions they would like to ask the composer about the piece of music and why?

Plenary:

Thank the children for all their thinking, sharing and good ideas. Say how well they co-operated and listened and how what they said showed that their thinking skills are amazing. Ask what they found interesting about the session.

Enrichment:

Some real live musicians!

Profile references:	Cross-curricular links for Foundation Stage:
LCT 1, 2, 3, and 5, 6, 7, 8, 9	DA 1, 6, 8
KS1 Core literacy: all those listed except those which specifically refer to 'text'.	SD 2, 3, 5, 5, 7, 9
	ED 3, 5, 7, 8, 9
	KUW 5; CD 7, 8
	KS1 - all topics, particularly music

Resources for thinking about the purpose of the arts

Some useful Paintings and Posters:

Pieter Breugel 'Peasant Wedding Feast' - lots of characters eating and being served.

The richness of variety and colour in paint with real-life observation of events is a feature of Breughel's paintings. The detail in his pictures often fascinates children.

- What would the sound be like if you could hear this picture?
- What would it smell like if you were in this painting?

Andy Goldsworthy (Google 'Andy Goldsworthy' in Google Images)

A sculptor working with natural materials, which he photographs before they are destroyed by the elements.

- Where do the artist's ideas come from?
- Some of these structures take a long time to make. How do you think he concentrates for so long? How do you make yourself concentrate?

Antony Gormley 'European Field' clay army.

This sculptor often uses clay body shapes, modelled on his own body, in large and small sizes for amazing effects.

- This artist often asks people to help him with his art (making clay figures) - does that make them artists too?

Wassily Kandinsky 'Cossacks' - three soldiers on horseback.

An abstract painting in colour, lines, shapes.

- What can you see in this painting?
- What might the artist be thinking when he was painting this picture?

Georges Seurat 'Sunday Afternoon on the Island of the Grande Jatte'.

A famous picture using Pointillism - painting with dots of pure colour.

- Look at the different characters in the painting - what might they be thinking?
- How long do you think it took to paint this picture?

Van Gogh 'The Potato Eaters'.

One of his studies and scenes painted in very thick paint.

- What might each of these people be thinking about?
- Where do you think they are (time and place)?

L.S. Lowry 'Coming from the Mill'.

A fascinating pictorial record, in muted colours painted straight onto the canvas, of industrial life in the north of England using his individual style.

- Where are all these people going?
- Choose a figure: what do you think this person   might be thinking?

Rene Magritte 'La Victoire' - an open door on a beach and cloud.

This surrealist painting is not all it seems to be.

- Why do you think the artist made this painting?
- What is happening?

Pablo Picasso 'Weeping Woman'.

A cubist painting where shapes are distorted and fragmented.

- Why do you think the woman is weeping?
- What does this painting make you think about?

Grant Wood 'American Gothic'.

This artist was inspired by, and painted, local surroundings and people in American life.

- Who are these people? (You could make up a story about them using clues from the picture).

Jackson Pollack 'Number 1A'.

This is one work by a famous action painter, who poured and threw paint on huge canvases.

- Is this a pattern or a picture? .
- What does this painting make you think of?

Kaffe Fassett patchwork fabrics, textiles, embroidery and knitting.

Amazing variety of colour and designs.

- Where do ideas come from?
- Can everyone have artistic ideas?

RSPB Images - a portfolio of natural world photos.

This wide variety of outdoor photos, clear and colourful is useful for all sorts of discussions.

- Why is there such a variety of life?
- How do you photograph animals without scaring them?

These paintings and pictures of these sculptures are all readily found on the web (for display on an interactive whiteboard or for purchase) by typing in the artists' name and paintings or sculptures.

Once the children are familiar with this method of looking at and discussing pictures they may enjoy looking at:

Tidying up Art - Ursus Wehrli - ISBN 3791330039

More Tidying up Art - ISBN 3039390058

An amusing look at art works stripped down to their dots and strokes.

Picture Poems - Michael and Peter Benton - ISBN 0340679875

Copies of paintings which are accompanied by the poems they inspired.

Willy's Pictures - Anthony Browne - ISBN 0744582407

An audacious look at art and chimpanzees!

See also the outline sessions on:

- Using art stimuli
- Using drawing as a stimulus
- Using picture cards as stimulus

Useful Artefacts to collect for use in 'Thinking about the Arts' sessions

- **Sculptures** made from all manner of media - marble, wood, clay - models of homes, people, animals, abstract.

- A wide variety of **musical instruments** including those from different cultures e.g. rain stick, tabla drum, ocarina, glockenspiel.

- **Ornaments**, vases, jewellery, knick-knacks, a giant marble - items which are interesting to touch - rough, smooth, shiny, bumpy, patterned, unusual, shiny, sequinned, ribboned.

- A variety of different **fabrics** from different cultures and made from different materials e.g. lengths of sari fabric or African printed material, floaty, thick.

- **Religious Artefact** - prayer mat, diva, Torah scroll, Celtic cross, turban, incense sticks.

- Objects from **other countries and cultures** e.g. Russian dolls, cuckoo clock, maps, boomerang, fans, masks - all the things people bring back from their holidays!

- **Historical objects** e.g. sugar tongs, butter and jelly moulds, bellows, scrubbing boards, a quill, a tin bath, some Roman coins.

- **Natural materials** - Leaves, conkers, twigs, herbs, perfumed flowers, fruits and vegetables, bark, rocks, shells, pebbles.

- **'Junk'**: collect things from bric-a-brac, White Elephant, jumble and rummage and car boot sales, museum shops, galleries, antique shops, pound shops, ethnic stores.

- It is well worth building up a **shared collection** of these resources (see Think about boxes in Section 2).

- You also might find the following useful when making collections:

  The Little Book of Treasure Baskets by Ann Roberts & Sally Featherstone

  and The Little Book of Treasure Boxes by Pat Brunton and Linda Thornton

Some Music to use as stimulation for Philosophy for Children

Some Music for Philosophical sessions:

'Air on a G string' Johann Sebastian Bach

'Cavalleria Rusticana - Intermezzo' Pietro Mascagni

'Cavatina' Stanley Myers

> These are haunting melodies
>
> • When do you think it would be appropriate to listen to this music?
>
> • What could be happening in a film with this music as the score?

'Peter and the Wolf' Sergei Prokofiev

> This music tells a story which children enjoy hearing
>
> • Why do you think Prokofiev chose these instruments to represent the characters in the story?
>
> • Would you have chosen these - or others?

'Harry Potter and the Philosopher's Stone' John Williams

'Lord of the Rings' theme tune Howard Shore

'Titanic' theme tune James Horner

> • You are going on an adventure: where might this music lead you?

Any Ladysmith Black Mambazo songs e.g. Izithembiso Zenkosi

> South African a cappella (unaccompanied) harmony singing

'The Journey: the best of Amadeus' or 'Amadeus' by Karl Jenkins

> Choirs singing 'world' lyrics
>
> • Why do people sing together?
>
> • How do you feel when you are singing?

'The Nutcracker Suite'

> Ballet music Peter Ilyich Tchaikovsky

Line Dance or Country Dance music

> • What makes people dance to music?
>
> • What would the world be like without music?

Thinking about poetry and stories

Title: Thinking about poetry
Group size: up to 12 children
Time: 15-20 minutes

Learning intention:

To encourage and develop thinking and speaking skills using a poem as a stimulus for ideas; to work cooperatively in a group.

Possible learning outcomes:

Children will be increasingly comfortable with thinking before they speak and keen to listen to other people's opinions and engage in discussion. They will learn to take turns to speak and use appropriate listening body language.

Resources:

Essential:

The book containing the poem to be shared *e.g.* Poems for the very Young edited by Michael Rosen which includes 'A Good Play' by Robert Louis Stevenson or 'Snow Thoughts'. (included on page 67)

Overview of the session:

The children hear the poem, then discuss what they think it is about, how it makes them think, and what questions they need to ask.

Main activity:

Welcome children to the thinking circle. Remind them of the rules for discussion.

'We are going to listen to a poem today and think and talk about it afterwards'.

Read the poem. Ask if anyone has any questions or comments that they would like to make about the poem. It is highly likely that the children will have lots to say and comment on but if they don't, you might like to suggest some questions for discussion.

Specific vocabulary	
poem	philosophy
poetry	speaking
beginning/middle	thinking
ending	listening
characters	responding
plot	ideas
illustrations	agree
poet	disagree
editor	opinion
collection	reflection
anthology	calm
publishers	quiet
pages	choose
verses	question
lines	open-ended

A Good Play (see next page) - What is the poem about?

How do you know it's a poem: what makes it a poem?

What does it mean when it says they had the 'very best of plays'?

How did they sail along for days and days?

As the children ask and answer these questions more will arise.

If there are too many for this session write then down for consideration at another time.

Snow Thoughts

Let's look at the questions in the poem and try to answer them!

Look at each line one by one.

Can you hear a rhyme?

Can a snowman do these four things (yes, if they are a magic snowman!).

What do you dream?

What do you think?

If there are too many questions for one session, write then down for consideration at another time.

Extension activity:

Use some extra time to keep on thinking and talking! - You could also vote on which question to discuss.

Plenary:

Talk with the children about what they found interesting in the poem. Thank them for thinking and sharing questions and good ideas. Talk about how they cooperated and listened, and how what they said showed their thinking skills. Ask what they found interesting about the session.

Enrichment:

Reading and sharing more poems from this book or other anthologies at the end of the session.

Profile references:
LCT 1, 2, 3, 4, 5, 6, 7, 8, 9
KS1 Core literacy: all those listed

Cross-curricular links for Foundation Stage:
DA 1, 6, 8   SD 2, 3, 5, 6, 7, 9
ED 3, 5, 7, 8   R 5   KUW 5

A Good Play

We built a ship upon the stairs
All made of the back-bedroom chairs
And filled it full of sofa pillows
To go a-sailing on the billows

We took a saw and several nails
And water in the nursery pails
And Tom said: 'Let us also take
An apple and a slice of cake;' -
Which was enough for Tom and me
To go a-sailing on till tea.

We sailed along for days and days
And had the very best of plays;
But Tom fell out and hurt his knee
So there was no-one left but me.

Robert Louis Stevenson

Snow Thoughts

What does a snowman eat?
What does a snowman drink?
What does a snowman dream?
What does a snowman think?

John Cunliffe

Title: Using stories for thinking
Group size: up to 12 children
Time: 15-20 minutes

Learning intention:
To encourage and develop thinking and speaking skills using a story as stimulus for ideas; to work cooperatively in a group.

Possible learning outcomes:
Children will be comfortable with thinking before they speak and keen to listen to other people's opinions and engage in discussion. They will take turns to speak and use appropriate listening body language.

Resources:
Essential:
A copy of a story book with potential for philosophical discussion - David McKee's 'Not Now, Bernard' or 'Where the Wild Things Are' by Maurice Sendak. Look at any of the books in your classroom and if you can ask a 'Why?' question about it it'll be alright!

Other suggestions: 'Wilfred Gordon Mcdonald Partridge' by Mem Fox, 'Dear Greenpeace' by Simon James, 'Oi, Get off our Train' by John Burningham

Overview of the session:
The children listen to the story with the understanding that they will be sharing a discussion about it. For the story telling it is useful for children to gather on the carpet, then return to the circle for the discussion.

Specific vocabulary		
story line	paperback	disagree
adventure	picture book	opinion
beginning	non-fiction	reflection
middle	pages	calm
ending	philosophy	quiet
characters	speaking	choose
plot	thinking	question
illustrations	listening	open-ended
author	responding	
publishers	ideas	
hard-back	agree	

Main activity:

Welcome children to the story/thinking/philosophy circle.

Remind them of the rules for discussion, recapping on why you need these rules.

Explain that you are going to share a story and do some thinking and talking about it afterwards.

Read the story, then ask the children to move to a talking circle, and ask some questions to help their thinking:

> What is strange about this story? Why did Bernard's parents behave like they did? Why did Bernard go to the monster if he thought it was going to eat him up? What makes a monster a monster?

Allow time for each child to speak if they wish to, and thank each person for their contribution. Act as a facilitator for the group, suggesting who speaks next but trying not to speak much yourself. Help the children to see where their views coincide or differ.

Extension activity:

When the children are very comfortable with this format for the session (this may take several sessions using different books), they need to move on to making a list of questions for discussion, voting for one and then discussing it. This takes time, and a longer session should be planned to allow for this. You will then be establishing a true 'community of enquiry' with the children having ownership of the whole process.

Plenary:

Talk with the children about what happened during the session. Discuss what worked well and what was difficult. Make sure everyone has a chance to contribute. Thank them for their concentration and the way they listened to other children's contributions.

Enrichment:

More time for discussion, and other stories

Profile references:	Cross-curricular links for Foundation Stage:
LCT 1, 2, 3, 4, 5, 6, 7, 8, 9	DA 1, 6, 8 SD 2, 3, 5, 6, 7, 9
KS1 Core literacy: all those listed	ED 3, 5, 7, 8, 9
	R 5
	KUW 5 CD 7
	KS1 - all topics

Three P4C sessions for very young children based on the story of Wilfred Gordon McDonald Partridge by Mem Fox

This is the story of a boy who visits and gets to know residents in an old people's home. He helps one resident to remember her youth with a collection of objects to remind her. He collected these ideas from other residents who have a variety of ideas about what 'memory' is.

Session 1

Begins with focus on objects in the centre of the circle, perhaps a swirl of fabric with picture cards of different people.

The adult says: 'Welcome to our philosophy (or thinking) session!'

Explain that you are going to look at the people pictures, and after a while each child will choose one to talk to everyone else about.

Remind the group of the Philosophy 'rules'

- Only one person talks at a time
- We signal when we have something to say (arm across body, resting on shoulder)
- We have a reason for what we say

Everyone sits quietly looking at the pictures for at least a minute.

Now allow everyone to choose a picture. It doesn't matter if more than one child picks the same picture, they can move to sit together, but each will need to think of something to say. If this does happen, give time for the pairs to discuss their contributions.

Go round the group with each person explaining why they chose that picture. Children might say:

- 'He's got a smiley face.' You could ask: 'Why do you think he's smiling?'
- 'She looks like me!' You could ask: 'How does she look like you?'
- 'He's very old.' You could ask: 'How do you know he is very old?'

Everyone can have something to say here that is their own opinion. Even the shyest person can be encouraged to say what they think.

Collect the pictures up, thank everyone, and finish with an action rhyme.

Session 2

Starts with a swirl of fabric too, but this time with the storybook in the centre, and chairs or mats in story telling mode (in a group so everyone can see the book).

Adult says 'Welcome! Today we are going to listen to and look at this story book'.

Read the story of Wilfred Gordon McDonald Partridge.

There are many opportunities throughout the story to involve the children in actions such as:

- 'Mrs. Jordan who played the organ' - (mime playing the organ - foot pedals as well!)
- 'Mrs. Hoskins who tells scary stories' (arms in the air like a monster - bare your teeth!)

Towards the end of the story the children will be able to join in the words as well as the actions!

Remind the group of the Philosophy 'rules'

- Only one person talks at a time
- We signal when we have something to say (arm across body, resting on shoulder).
- We have a reason for what we say

The adult then suggests that the group talk about who they liked in the story and why, and explains that everyone can have a turn if they want to.

Go round the group with each person explaining what they liked about the story. Children might say:

- 'I liked Mr. Tippet who was crazy about cricket - because I am too!'

Remember that everyone's contribution is valid, and encourage them to say WHY they liked the person and what they did.

End with an action song such as 'There Was a Princess Long ago...'

Session 3

This also needs a swirl of fabric with 6 objects for Kim's game, for example, an apple, an orange, a banana, a shell, a piece of jewellery, a shiny pebble

The adult says 'Welcome! Today we are going to see how good you are at remembering, like the people in our story last week'.

Explain that everyone is going to look at the objects and then you are going to cover them up with a thick cloth that hides lumps and bumps.

'As a group we are going to work together to try to remember what is under the cloth.' some older children might want to try on their own.

Remind the group of the Philosophy 'rules'
- Only one person talks at a time

- We signal when we have something to say (arm across body, resting on shoulder)

- We have a reason for what we say

After enjoying this game together, remind children of the story, and encourage them to re-cap in their own words, perhaps with actions.

'Now we are going to talk about this question - What is memory?'

Allow thinking time for everyone with out interrupting, then encourage everyone to have a turn.

Finish the session with an action song such as 'Heads, Shoulders, Knees and Toes.'

By the end of these three sessions, the children will begin to understand the expectations and routine of a P4C activity. These first sessions have been very much adult-led, but the aim is for everyone to have confidence in running the sessions and this structure may help you to get started.

Poetry for Philosophy for Children

Delightful and very useful collections which can be used time and again are:

Wriggle and Roar! Rhymes to join in with - Julia Donaldson ISBN 1405021667
Poems for the Very Young - Edited by Michael Rosen ISBN 1856971163
Don't put Mustard in the Custard - Michael Rosen ISBN 0439981417
All Join in - Quentin Blake ISBN 009926353X
First Poems for Thinking - Robert Fisher ISBN 189825530X
Peace Begins with Me; A Collection of Poems Edited by Jill Bennett ISBN 019276232X
Pass the Jam, Jim - Kaye Umansky ISBN 009926344
Picture Poems - Michael and Peter Benton ISBN 0340679875
Puffin Book of Fantastic First Poems - Edited by June Crebbin ISBN 0141308982
The Puffin Book of Twentieth-century Children's Verse - edited by Brain Patten ISBN 0140322361

Some nursery rhymes make good discussion topics: 'Twinkle, Twinkle, Little star' even asks its own philosophical question! You can certainly try to understand something of what might seem nonsense in nursery rhymes by asking open questions about them and enjoying thinking of answers.

- 3 Blind Mice
- Baa Baa Black Sheep
- Goosey Goosey Gander
- Hickory Dickory Dock
- Humpty Dumpty
- Incy Wincey Spider
- Jack and Jill
- Jack be Nimble
- Little Bo Peep
- Little Miss Muffet
- Mary, Mary, Quite Contrary
- The Grand Old Duke of York

- Old Mother Hubbard
- Polly Put the Kettle on
- Ride a Cock Horse
- Ring a Ring of Roses
- See Saw Margery Daw
- Sing a Song of Sixpence
- Twinkle, Twinkle
- Wee Willie Winkie

The illustrations in these anthologies might give some clues about the ideas in the rhymes:
- Lucy Cousins' Big Book of Nursery Rhymes ISBN 0333726698
- Nicola Bailey's Book of Nursery Rhymes ISBN 1900465963
- A Child's Garden of Verses; Robert Louis Stevenson ISBN 159572057X

Useful books for story stimulus

'A Dark, Dark Tale' Ruth Brown ISBN 0803716737
Issues: Being scared in the dark, adventure, suspense
Questions: Is it OK to show you are scared?
Why do we sometimes do things which scare ourselves?

'All Kinds of Beliefs' Emma Damon ISBN 1857075056
Issues: People's different beliefs and life positions
Questions: Why doesn't everyone believe the same things?
Can you believe in nothing?

'All Kinds of Bodies' Emma Damon ISBN 1857075609
Issues: Size, shape, differences, similarities
Questions: Are some people's bodies better than others?
Is variety good?

'All Kinds of People' Emma Damon ISBN 9781857070675
Issues: Skin colour, disability, differences, similarities
Questions: How can so many different people live in harmony?
What is a 'normal' person like?

'Always and Forever' Alan Durant ISBN 038560503X
Issues: Friendship, failings, death, remembrance
Questions: What qualities make a friend?
Why should we celebrate someone's life?

'Ask Me' Antje Damm ISBN 184507386X
This amazing book has a picture and question on each page to stimulate philosophical thinking e.g. 'What do you wish that could never come true?'
Who do YOU teach?
Do you think you have a guardian angel?

'Dear Greenpeace' Simon James ISBN 0744530601
Issues: The environment, citizenship, getting involved
Questions: Do one person's efforts count for anything?
Was there really a whale in the pond?

'Dinosaurs and all that Rubbish' Michael Foreman ISBN 9780140552607
Issues: Pollution, responsibility, the future, the past
Questions: Why did he want to go to the star?
Can having lots of money get you what you want?

'Dogger' Shirley Hughes ISBN 009992790X
Issues: Special things, losing and finding, love
Questions: Why are we upset when we lose things?
Why are we happy when we find things?

'First Stories for Thinking' Robert Fisher ISBN 1898255296
There are 30 stories in this book all with lots of questions; a good investment!

'Granpa' John Burningham ISBN 0099434083
Issues: Old and young, companionship, death and loss
Questions: What did the boy and his grandpa share which was so special?
How will the boy cope without his grandpa?

'Handa's Surprise' Eileen Browne ISBN 0744536340
Issues: Surprises, anticipation
Questions: How do you think Handa will explain the satsumas when she didn't notice anything happening? What makes a good surprise?

'How to Catch a Star' Oliver Jeffers ISBN 0007150334
Issues: Patience, illusion
Questions: What can we do about something we really want? Is wanting something the same as needing something?

'I am too Absolutely Small for School' Lauren Child ISBN 184362366-8
Issues: New challenges, fears
Questions: Why is Lola afraid of school? How can we help someone who is afraid?

'I Want a Friend' Tony Ross ISBN 184270298X
Issues: Loneliness, making friends
Questions: How can we make friends with someone? How can you be a friend?

'I'm Sorry' Sam McBratney ISBN 0006646298
Issues: Friendship, quarrels, making up, saying sorry
Questions: Why is it so hard to say sorry? What makes us fall out with our best friends?

'Is it Right to Fight?' Pat Thomas ISBN 0750242620
Issues: Aggression, ways to live peaceably
Questions: Ask the question in the title: Is it right to fight? How can we live peacefully?

'Love you for Ever' Robert Munsch ISBN 009926689X
Issues: Life cycles, love, parenthood, childhood
Questions: Did his mum really want to sell him to the zoo? Why did the song always say 'my baby you'll be' even when he was grown up?

'Michael Rosen's Sad Book' ISBN 0744598982
Issues: Depression, death, being positive, being negative
Questions: Why are we so unhappy when someone dies? How can we help someone who is very sad?

'Night Monkey, Day Monkey' Julia Donaldson ISBN 0749748931
Issues: Understanding, difference
Questions: What does it feel like to be confused? How can we prevent ourselves from being confused?

'Not Now Bernard' David McKee ISBN 0099240505
Issues: Monsters, parents, true, imagination
Questions: What are monsters? Why do parent sometimes not notice us?

'No Worries' Marcia Williams ISBN 0744577543
Issues: Being worried,
Questions: Why do people worry even when there seems to be nothing to worry about? How do you deal with worries?

'Oi, Get off our Train' John Burningham ISBN 009985340X
Issues: Wildlife, extinction, imagination,
Questions: How did the boy go on this adventure? What will the world be like if animals become extinct?

'Once There Were Giants' Penny Dale ISBN 0744578361
Issues: Being born, growing up, being adult
Questions: Does everyone have giants?
What do you think it will be like being giant?

'One World' Michael Foreman ISBN 0862642892
Issues: Pollution, responsibility, sharing and caring of resources
Questions: What can we do about pollution?

'Owl Babies' Martin Waddell ISBN 0744531675
Issues: Fear, uncertainty, not knowing
Questions: What can we do when we are afraid of something?
Is it ever useful to be afraid?

'Rosie the Hen' Pat Hutchins ISBN 009941399X
Issues: Fear, safety, ignorance
Questions: Why did Rosie never see the fox chasing her?
Why did the fox never succeed in catching Rosie?

'Selfish Sophie' Damian Kelleher ISBN 0749643854
Issues: Selfishness, loneliness
Questions: Are we sometimes selfish?
Do we have to share?

'Something Beautiful' Sharon Dennis Wyeth
ISBN 0440412102
Issues: Beauty, ugliness,
Questions: What is the 'something beautiful' in your life?
How can we make beauty?

'Tadpole's Promise' Jeanne Willis and Tony Ross
ISBN 1842700693
Issues: Promises, apologies, change, life cycles
Questions: Did the creatures have to change?

Why are we shocked at the end of the story?
'The Colour of Home' Mary Hoffman
ISBN 0711219400
Issues: Asylum seekers, fear, sorrow, sharing
Questions: How do people cope with sad memories?
Can we help people to cope with sad memories?

'The Conquerors' David McKee ISBN 1842703307
Issues: Power, invasions, peaceable people
Questions: How powerful is it being peaceful?
Why do some people want to bully?

'The Patchwork Quilt' Valerie Flournoy
ISBN 0140554335
Issues: Remembering, becoming old, memories, skill
Questions: How do we remember things from the past?
Do we need to remember things from the old days?

'The Rainbow Fish' Marcus Pfister ISBN 1558580093
Issues: Friendship, sharing, vanity
Questions: Do we all need friends or can we manage without?
Is everyone vain in some way?

'The Selfish Giant' Oscar Wilde ISBN 0140503838
Issues: Selfishness, sadness, greed
Questions: Why was the giant selfish?
Does selfishness always lead to pain?

'The Very Hungry Caterpillar' Eric Carle
ISBN 0140500871
Issues: Feasting, change, life-cycles
Questions: Do we need caterpillars in our world?
What happens when people are greedy?

'What is Peace?' Emma Damon ISBN 1857076567
Issues: Being positive, hopeful,
Questions: Think of the question in the title: What is
peace?
What is the opposite of peace?

'When I was Little' Marcia Williams ISBN 0744517656
Issues: History, memory, imagination
Questions: Will it ever be like Grandma's world again?
How did they manage without all the modern things?

'Where the Wild Things Are' Maurice
Sendak
ISBN 0099408392
Issues: Imagination,
monsters,
Questions: Were the
monsters real?
How do we know
when we are
dreaming?

'Wilfred Gordon McDonald Partridge' Mem Fox
ISBN 0140505865
Issues: Memory, old age, youth, friendships,
generations
Questions: What is memory?
Why did everyone think memories were different?

'Willie the Wimp' Andrew Browne ISBN 0744543630
Issues: Bravery, cowardice, friendship
Questions: Does it matter what size you are?
What are you brave about?

'Za-za's Baby Brother' Lucy Cousins ISBN 0744570263
Issues: Family life, sibling rivalry, attention-seeking,
patience
Questions: What does it feel like to be ignored?

Using persona dolls for P4C

Persona Dolls are primarily a tool for teaching, learning and understanding about similarities and differences between people. Persona Dolls are a great asset in the teaching of PSHCE and RE if your setting or school community contains a limited range of cultures. Learning about someone's life or faith through a persona doll helps make different experiences and beliefs real and relevant to young children. It is best to keep notes on the doll's persona and scenarios tackled through them, and keep collecting information about different cultures, disabilities, backgrounds, behaviours, self-esteem or special needs - there is always something new to explore using a Persona Doll.

Using the dolls regularly becomes as easy as doing any Circle Time activity. It allows the children to think questions through, coming up with good observations, as long as we give them time to process their thoughts and ideas. Any doll can be used, but a realistic 'child,' rather than a baby doll is best. Avoid character dolls such as Barbie, Action Man, as they come with stereotypical characteristics.

You only need one doll to get started, and it is a very good way to ensure that children really are learning about 'Personal, Social and Emotional Development' and 'Knowledge and Understanding of the World'.

The dolls can be used to:

- help children anticipate and prepare for new learning;
- help children understand and deal with their own daily fears, anxieties, pleasures, disappointments;
- help children to cope with new situations, feelings, family events, lifestyle changes;
- help children to challenge unfairness, bias and discrimination.

Useful resources:

'The Little Book of Persona Dolls' by Marilyn Bowles (Featherstone Education)

A Useful DVD 'Celebrating Diversity' can be ordered from the inter-active and user-friendly web site: www.persona-doll-training.org

Title: Thinking with a persona doll - it's not fair
Group size: up to 12 children
Time: 15-20 minutes

Learning intention:
To think, talk, listen and respond to the issue of 'It's not fair!'.

Possible learning outcomes:
Children will begin to empathise with people with special needs, how they may be treated differently, and begin to understand why.

Resources:
Essential:
A Persona doll - this can be any doll which the children do not play with, except during persona doll sessions. A photo could be substituted, but the children identify very well with a doll character, so it is well worth buying one.

Overview of the session:
The adult will introduce the children to the persona doll with a brief discussion of their name and something about them.

Then they will introduce the issue of what it feels like to be a new person or in a new situation, and share ideas of how to can help that person.

The doll will 'tell' the children, through the adult, that they know a person in their class who has a problem with their behaviour, and they are allowed to do all sorts of things that the doll character is not, such as shouting out in the hall, walking round at story times, banging doors, playing a drum over and over again when it should be quiet time, and the doll thinks 'It's not fair!'.

The children will be asked 'What do you think?'

Specific vocabulary
name of the persona doll
feel
think
how
why
when
nerves
(re)assurance

Main activity:

Welcome the children to the group, and say 'We have a visitor today who would like your help' and bring in the Persona doll. Don't keep the doll squashed in a bag, or under a chair, give them a real place and treat them like a real visitor.

Introduce the doll by name and say why s/he is here. The doll knows a person in their class who has special needs, and they are allowed to do all sorts of things that s/he is not - like shout out in the hall, walk around at story times, bang doors, play a drum over and over again when it should be quiet and play outside when they have to write and they think 'It's not fair!' Say 'What do you think?'

Share ideas:

You may need to explain that people who have special needs think differently from other people and often do unusual things which they can't help doing. Perhaps they could explain this to the doll, and encourage them to be patient and understanding. Talk about how difficult this must be for the class - have they any ideas to help? Encourage the children to contribute any ideas they have - and try not to be too judgmental if you don't agree with them!

Extension activity:

Read 'That's not fair!' by Carol Peters, Leicester City Council, Special Needs Department. Discuss the book together.

Plenary:

Thank the children for all their good suggestions and help for the doll. Discuss how you could all help someone who is new or different. Allow the children to recap and list the suggestions that have been so helpful. Say goodbye to the visitor (you could pass the doll round the circle for goodbyes) and say that you hope that their ideas will be helpful.

Enrichment:

A member of staff or an older child could be willing to be involved in this situation. It is not appropriate to use a peer of the children in the group. This gets in the way of objective thinking and may result in a child being labelled.

Profile references:	Cross-curricular links for Foundation Stage:
LCT 1, 2, 6, 7, 8	DA 1 SD 4 ED 4, 5
KS1 Core literacy: all those listed except those which specifically refer to 'text'.	KUW 6
	KS1 - all topics

Section Five - The Outcomes

Learning outcomes for children involved in P4C

There are many learning outcomes for young children when they are trying philosophy in this way. Here are some:

Reflection

Quality time should be planned to allow for reflection, and for children to hear what others are thinking, so they can reflect on that too. This unhurried approach, with times of peace and quiet can be an oasis of calm for children.

Listening skills

Opportunities to learn how to listen, to look at the person who is speaking and to adopt listening body language may help some children to be able to do, hear and understand what others are saying to them.

Thinking

Because the thinking is focused and has a direct purpose, the discussion that emerges will be purposeful and helpful, and children will be encouraged to keep on task.

Developing respect for other people and their differences

Respect is an important and difficult ability for young children to develop. Understanding that we can have views that are different from others, and they can have views different from ours takes time and commitment. Learning that difference is OK, and that differences should be respected without arguing or losing your temper is hard, but well worth the effort!

Engaging with new ideas

Some children have limited or extreme life experiences, and everyone in the group needs to understand and engage with the concept that life is different for different people. Children will bring their own home experiences and parents views with them and can sometimes feel challenged when meeting others with different views. Allow the time and space for these problems and conflicts to be discussed and resolved.

Emotional literacy

Opportunities to explore big issues inevitably leads to a wider understanding of them. Talking about and sharing views which are not yet fully thought out enables them to be clarified and

Extending language, complexity of grammar, vocabulary and articulation

The development and improvement of language are added bonuses of the strategy. Language for thinking and language for communication are practiced each time P4C is tried out, and opportunities to experiment with language will be handled sympathetically - an ideal way to learn.

Working collaboratively

The EYFS has key outcomes for working together, and the Primary Framework has a core learning grid for literacy **'group discussion and interaction.'** This is one of the purposes of P4C too, and the overlap will ensure that all children have plenty of opportunities to develop the necessary skills.

Raising self-esteem

Having an idea which finds favour with your peers is a powerful feeling for anyone. Having someone say 'I agree with you.....' is quite something. Having someone say they disagree with you is also acceptable if it is done with tact and diplomacy the P4C way.

Improving reasoning skills

It is easy to have an opinion of someone or something but much harder to define why you think this. Listening to others trying to do this in P4C sessions gives clues and ideas to help clarify and explain why you think what you do.

Taking turns

In a busy world when everyone is clamouring to be heard, a structured turn-taking setting is a real oasis of calm and order, with everyone having an equal right to speak and be heard.

Constructing and developing an argument

This is a skill which even adults struggle with daily - perhaps an earlier start will help children in the future!

Outcomes for facilitators

There is a wonderful personal satisfaction in encouraging children to take part in philosophy sessions because they blossom with the opportunities to share their thoughts and ideas. Listening to the children helps the adult to learn about their language development and about their personal lives and thinking. Likewise, the children learn about each other. It is also fun to see that on many occasions the children can be shown to be more aware and switched on than the adults, showing originality and insight, and the ability to think creatively.

Every child can have an element of personalisation, they can work at their own ability level, and learn from others too. Emotional literacy is the ability to conduct oneself appropriately in any situation, being aware of others, careful of the situation and thoughtful. This type of creative thinking and responding to the emotions of others should be a regular part of the day and the week, so children develop into thoughtful and caring adults.

This circle of talk allows dialogue across the group, with everyone having an opportunity to speak and explore open-ended questions.

We all need to balance the pressure of ensuring pace in sessions with the need for time and space for thinking and internalising experiences. We need to be prepared for a silence while children put together their thoughts or repeat an idea already expressed.

Parents and P4C

Parents should be encouraged to understand the purpose of your philosophy sessions, and an invitation to join one of your sessions is one way to help them understand what is going on. Children are taught many subjects as a series of facts and a good memory is a terrific bonus in factual recall, but thinking is a much more difficult skill to qualify and assess. Problem-solving, creativity and cooperation can be seen, but are much more difficult to measure!

'I and other adults who engage in philosophical dialogues with children on a regular basis have found again and again that children of all learning levels, and of all social and economic backgrounds excel in the fourth 'r' - the ability to reason. Their sense of self is strengthened, and as a result they are more motivated to develop their abilities in the traditional three Rs.'

Christopher Phillips, teacher of Socratic Dialogue www.philosopher.org

P4C - observing and assessing

It is delightful to watch children blossoming when engaged in philosophy sessions: what they say is so often memorable, and a useful insight into their knowledge and understanding of a much wider curriculum then the basics of literacy and numeracy.

Some assessment criteria which parents might be encouraged to share might include:

- Offers an opinion in a few words
- Contributions are relevant to the topic
- Offers an opinion and reason if asked
- Answers in sentences
- Uses expression in their voice and face
- Shows group empathy and participates well
- Listens to the contributions of others
- Talks about their feelings
- Uses listening body language
- Can express an opinion different to others'
- Can accept differences

'Opinions are not facts.
What happened and how you feel about it are two different things.
And people should know which is which.'

www.theguardian.co.uk

Section Six
Find out more

Organisations which promote Philosophy for Children:

SAPERE - Society for Advancing Philosophical Enquiry and Reflection in Education

Oxford Brookes University, Harcourt Hill, OXFORD, OX2 9AT

Membership of SAPERE provides regular newsletters, gives advice about training and organises conferences and regional networks. SAPERE became a registered charity in 1991 after a BBC documentary on 'Philosophy for Children'. They offer training at 3 levels, and support implementation in schools, e.g. demonstration lessons and teacher coaching. SAPERE provide the only accredited courses in the UK www.sapere.org.uk

DialogueWorks gives training to teachers in schools and at courses and events. www.dialogueworks.co.uk

Teaching Thinking and Creativity Journal - by Imaginative Minds ISSN 14706105

This magazine is packed with articles from teachers and researchers who are exploring ways to engage children in thinking creatively. They 'focus on practical principles for creativity and report on exciting projects and innovation in schools, providing resources that teachers need to make education more imaginative and effective.' They also produce a catalogue of useful books and resources covering issues such as 'Thinking and Literacy,' 'Gifted and Talented Learners,' 'Creativity across the Curriculum'.

Persona Dolls - a strategy which looks at a variety of life stances and encourages discussion about similarities and differences, problem-resolution and empathy. The use of dolls gives a focus for the group as they debate the issues. The children develop amazing empathy with the dolls even though they know that is exactly what they are. It enables very pertinent subjects to be discussed without subjecting individual people to a spotlight.

www.persona-doll-training.org provides training and a range of resources, including dolls from many cultures.

See also: **The Little Book of Persona Dolls** by Marilyn Bowles ISBN 1-904187-86-2

Some books

Storywise: Thinking through Stories by Karin Murris and Joanna Haynes
Published by DialogueWorks as:

Storywise Starter Pack ISBN 1903804000 and

Storywise Teachers' Guidance ISBN 1903804019 (This resource explores ways to use many quality picture story books for philosophy sessions.)

Let me be Peter Dixon ISBN 1873195125 poems and reflections

Toxic Childhood Sue Palmer ISBN 0752873598

Detoxing Childhood Sue Palmer ISBN 0752890107

The Little Book of Listening Clare Beswick ISBN 1904187692

The Little Book of Circle Time Dawn Roper ISBN 1904187943

The Little Book of Story Telling Mary Medlicott ISBN 190418765X

The Thinking Child Resource Book Nicola Call with Sally Featherstone; Network Continuum Press Ltd. ISBN 1855391619

The Thinking Child Nicola Call with Sally Featherstone published by Network Educational Press Ltd. ISBN 185539121X

Thinking Skills (Ages 4-5) Georgie Beasley published by Scholastic Ltd. ISBN 043998338X

The Effective Provision of Pre-School Education (EPPE) **Project** - Iram Siraj-Blatchford (London Institute of Education) revealed evidence that 'sustained shared thinking' and 'open-ended questioning' extended children's thinking and improve their attainment at school.

Glossary and Foundation Stage Profile and KS1 Core Learning in Literacy

Community of Enquiry: a group of people used to thinking together with a view to increasing their understanding and appreciation of the world around them and each other.

Creative thinking: able to see and make things in a new and different way.

Critical thinking: clear, precise and purposeful thinking: solving complex problems but also the evaluation of one's own thinking: synthesising.

Descriptive questioning: what? when? why? where? who? when? how?

Emotional literacy: the ability to conduct oneself appropriately to the situation; being aware and careful of the situation: being thoughtful. A type of creative thinking responding to the emotions of others, supporting others. Explored by Daniel Goleman.

Emotional illiteracy: pub squabbles, hooliganism, vandalism.

Facilitator: the person who enables the enquiry to move on: in well-established groups this could be a child. It involves managing fairness of opportunity in the group and adherence to the group rules.

Opinion: the ideas and beliefs that a person has about something, usually based on their own experience of life.

Philosophy: philo- the love of sophy- wisdom and through philosophical enquiry we can consider the nature of our being, and the world in which we live.

Pole-bridging: talking about what you are doing when you are doing an activity alongside a child.

Reflection: consideration of ideas.

Reflective questioning: How did it feel? What did it make you wonder? Why do you think that happened?

Socratic dialogue: conversations with questions and answers.

Speculative questioning: What if...? What might happen next? What might the person be thinking? What question might they ask? What would you do?

Synthesis: putting together of ideas.

P4C links with the Foundation Stage Profile / Curriculum
Personal, Social and Emotional Development links:

Dispositions and Attitudes

DA1	Shows an interest in classroom activities through observation and participation
DA6	Continues to be interested, motivated and excited to learn
DA7	Is confident to try new activities, initiate ideas and speak in a familiar group
DA8	Maintains attention and concentrates
DA9	Sustains involvement and perseveres, particularly when trying to solve a problem or reach a satisfactory solution

Social Development

SD2	Builds relationships through gesture and talk
SD3	Takes turns and shares with adult support
SD4	Works as part of a group, taking turns and sharing fairly
SD5	Forms good relationships with adults and peers
SD6	Understands that there need to be agreed values and codes of behaviour for groups of people, including adults and children, to work together harmoniously
SD7	Understands that people have different needs, views, cultures and beliefs that need to be treated with respect
SD8	Understands that s/he can expect others to treat her or his needs, views, cultures and beliefs with respect
SD9	Takes into account the ideas of others

Emotional Development

ED1	Takes initiatives and manages developmentally appropriate task. Separates from main carer with support
ED2	Shows a strong sense of self as a member of different communities, such as his/her family setting. Communicates freely about home and community
ED3	Expresses needs and feelings in appropriate ways
ED4	Responds to significant experiences, showing a range of feelings when appropriate
ED5	Has a developing awareness of own needs, views and feelings and is sensitive to the needs, views and feelings of others
ED6	Has a developing respect for own culture and beliefs and those of other people
ED7	Considers the consequences of words and actions for self and others
ED8	Understands what is right, what is wrong, and why
ED9	Displays a strong and positive sense of self-identity and is able to express a range of emotions fluently and appropriately

Communication, Language and Literacy links:

Language for Communication and Thinking

LCT1	Listens and responds
LCT2	Initiates communication with others, displaying greater confidence in more formal contexts
LCT3	Talks activities through, reflecting on and modifying actions
LCT4	Listens with enjoyment to stories, songs, rhymes and poems, sustains attentive listening and responds with relevant comments, questions and actions

LCT5	Uses language to imagine and recreate roles and experiences
LCT6	Interacts with others in a variety of contexts, negotiating plans and activities and taking turns in conversation
LCT7	Uses talk to organise, sequence and clarify thinking, ideas, feelings and events, exploring the meanings and sound of new words
LCT8	Speaks clearly with confidence and control, showing an awareness of the listener
LCT9	Talks and listens confidently and with control, consistently showing awareness of the listener by including relevant detail. Uses language to work out and clarify ideas, showing a range of appropriate vocabulary.

Reading

R1	Is developing an interest in books
R2	Knows that print carries meaning
R5	Shows an understanding of the elements of stories, such as main character, sequence of events and openings
R8	Shows an understanding of how information can be found in non-fiction texts to answer questions about where, who, why and how

Knowledge and Understanding of the World

KUW3	Identifies obvious similarities and differences when exploring and observing. Constructs in a purposeful way, using simple tools and techniques
KUW4	Investigates places, objects, materials and living things by using all the senses as appropriate. Add: Identifies some features and talks about those features s/he likes/dislikes
KUW5	Asks questions about why things happen and how things work. Looks closely at similarities and differences, patterns and change.

KUW6	Finds out about past and present events in own life, and in those of family members and other people s/he knows. Begins to know about own culture and belief and those of other people
KUW7	Finds out about and uses everyday technology and uses information and communication technology and programmable toys to support his/her learning

Creative Development

CD5	Explores colour, texture, shape, form and space in two and three dimensions
CD7	Uses imagination in art and design, music, dance, imaginative and role-play and stories. Responds in a variety of ways to what s/he sees, hears, smells, touches and feels
CD8	Expresses and communicates ideas, thoughts and feelings using a range of materials, suitable tools, imaginative and role-play, movement, designing and making, and a variety of songs and musical instruments
CD9	Expresses feelings and preferences in response to artwork, drama and music and makes some comparisons and links between different pieces. Responds to own work and that of others when exploring and communicating ideas, feelings and preferences through art, music, dance, role play and imaginative play.

Primary Framework for Literacy 2006
Core Learning in Literacy by Year
These are links used in the philosophy session examples

In Year 1 most children should learn to:

Speaking	• Tell stories and describe incidents from their own experience in an audible voice • Interpret a text by reading aloud with some variety of pace and emphasis
Listening and Responding	• Listen to and follow instructions accurately, asking for help and clarification if necessary
Group Discussion and interaction	• Takes turns to speak, listen and to others' suggestions and talk about what they are going to do • Ask and answer questions, make relevant contributions, offer suggestions and take turns • Explain their views to others in a small group, decide how to report the group's views to the class
Drama	• Discuss why they like a performance
Understanding and Interpreting texts	• Make predictions showing an understanding of ideas, vents and characters
Engaging with and Responding to texts	• Visualise and comment on events, characters and ideas, making imaginative links to their own experience

In Year 2 most children should learn to:

Speaking	• Tell real and imagined stories using the conventions of familiar story language • Explain processes using imaginative and adventurous vocabulary and non-verbal gestures to support communication
Listening and Responding	• Listen to others in class, ask relevant questions and follow instructions
Group Discussion and interaction	• Ensure that everyone contributes, allocates tasks, and considers alternatives and reach agreement • Work effectively in groups by ensuring that each group member takes a turn challenging, supporting and moving on • Listens to each other's views and preferences, agree the next steps to take and identify contributions made by each group member
Drama	• Adopt appropriate roles on small or large groups and consider different courses of action
Understanding and Interpreting texts	• Gives some reasons why things happen or characters change
Engaging with and Responding to texts	• Explain their reactions to texts, commenting on important aspects

The contents of this book have also been informed be reading a range of articles and publications particularly about the work of Matthew Lipman, Robert Fisher, Karen Murris and Lev Vygotsky, the internet sites of universities and other organisations across the world.

Other titles in the Key Issues series

Boys & Girls Come Out to Play

ISBN 978-1-905019-17-5

Ros Bayley and Sally Featherstone have collaborated once more to follow their successful book Smooth Transitions with this exploration of the differences in brain development, learning and behaviour between girls and boys in the Foundation Stage and Key Stage 1.

Running and Racing

ISBN 978-1-905019-18-2

Keep on the move with this book which is based on established research and current guidance on child health and fitness. The suggested activities are easy to fit into your programme, need minimal equipment and are fun for children and adults alike.

Sustaining Shared Thinking

ISBN 978-1-905019-89-2

What are thinking skills? How do they develop? What can adults do to help children acquire them? This book contains plenty of ideas and suggestions for ways to challenge and interest children, engage their brains and support them in reasoning, solving problems and developing their powers of thought.

This important new series addresses some of the major issues facing early years settings and primary schools. The aim is to provide sound, clear advice, based on extensive knowledge and supported by the latest research. All the authors are experienced teachers and practitioners.

The series editor is Sally Featherstone.

The Key Issues strands are

- **Transfer, continuity & progression**
- **Gender issues**
- **Fitness & health**
- **Diet & nutrition**
- **A sense of identity**

Key Issues are available from www.acblack.com/featherstone